Other titles by Charles A. Mendenhall:

Delta Wings: Convair's High-Speed Planes Of The Fifties & Sixties
Deadly Duo: The B-25 And B-26 In WWII
The Gee Bee Racers

WILDCATS & HELLCATS

Gallant Grummans In World War II

CHARLES A. MENDENHALL

Osceola, Wisconsin 54020, USA

ISBN: 0-87938-177-9
Library of Congress Number: 83-27231

Printed and bound in the United States of America.
Book and cover design by William F. Kosfeld.
Cover photograph by Budd Davisson.

1 2 3 4 5 6 7 8 9 10

Library of Congress Cataloging in Publication Data

Mendenhall, Charles A.
Wildcats & Hellcats.

Bibliography: p.
Includes index.
1. Wildcat (Fighter plane)—History. 2. Hellcat (Fighter planes)—History. 3. United States. Navy—Aviation—History—20th century. 4. World War, 1939–1945—Aerial operations, American. 5. World War, 1939–1945—Naval operations, American. I. Title. II. Title: Wildcats and Hellcats.
UG1242.F5M46 1984 358.4'3 83-27231
ISBN 0-87938-177-9 (pbk.)

INTRODUCTION

From Eugene Ely, dressed in football helmet and inflated bicycle inner tubes, fluttering from the eighty-three-foot flight ramp of the USS *Birmingham* to the F-14A Tomcat, blasting off the nuclear carrier *Enterprise* was a long process. About midpoint through that evolution were the memorable Grumman F4F Wildcat and F6F Hellcat carrier fighters of World War II. It had not been long after the Wrights' big event at Kill Devil Hill that the idea of making a waterbird of the new flying machine had sprung up. Interest was in two directions; taking off and landing on the water or, more to the subject in this book, taking off and landing on a ship's deck.

Eugene Ely was not "Navy." He was, rather, a young and daring exhibition flyer of the early days of stick, wire and canvas who had gained attention flying with the Curtiss team during the International Air Meet at Belmont Park, New York, in October 1910. In November he went on to make some splashy headlines by performing the first successful takeoff from a ship. To help that cause along, a small wooden ramp had been constructed on the light cruiser USS *Birmingham*, anchored at Hampton Roads, Virginia, for the trial. The ramp was slanted at five degrees for a downhill takeoff. His Curtiss Model D airplane was fitted with wing-mounted canister floats and, to really make sure it floated, a bag of corks was tied under the fuselage framework! The aircraft, called the *Albany Flier*, had demonstrated its range and airworthiness during Glenn Curtiss' noteworthy flight from Albany to New York City in May of the same year.

Ely, with his nose wheel a scant fifty-seven feet from the drop-off of the twenty-four-foot-wide ramp, fired up the clattering engine and trundled off the deck's edge into thin air. Gaining airspeed was a horserace with the deck's altitude of thirty-seven feet. Ely came close to not winning. The propeller tips, flotation canisters, fuselage frame and wheels all skipped off the water's surface before the *Albany Flier* became airborne. The propeller was banged up and caused the aircraft to severely vibrate. Ely headed for Willoughby Spit, the nearest land, two-and-a-half miles away. The close call confirmed in some minds that a sort of catapult might be a better way to go. The aircraft could then gain suitable flying speed before leaving a ship's deck. It was good thinking and the idea's day would come.

Nevertheless, the first half of the shipboard flight equation was now solved. One could take off—but, how about landing? Ely was drafted again and a new trial was set up on San Francisco Bay for a landing attempt on January 18, 1911. This time the wooden flight ramp was somewhat larger, thirty-two feet wide and 120 feet long. It was constructed on the stern of the cruiser USS *Pennsylvania*. A lip on the deck canted downward over the ship's stern to accept the plane if the approach was a trifle low. Canvas sheets were draped over the ship's aft superstructure and along either side of the wooden landing ramp. These were to act as safety barriers in case of an accidental overrun during the landing attempt.

Twenty-two evenly spaced ropes were stretched across the ramp. They were attached at either end to fifty-pound sandbags. The ropes were also propped up a few inches above the ramp surface so that arresting hooks attached to the aircraft's landing gear could easily engage them and drag the Curtiss D-IV to a stop. The aircraft was again equipped with the flotation canisters and Ely with the football helmet and inflated bicycle inner tubes.

Lifeguards and lifeboats stood by in case the trial should become a fiasco, with Ely and plane in the water. Ely took off from the airfield at San Francisco's Presidio and, pushed along by a mild tailwind, soon came in sight of the *Pennsylvania*'s waiting observers. He carefully made his final approach, coming in over the end of the ramp at about forty miles per hour. The landing gear hooks caught the ropes. Pilot and plane came to a stop with fifty feet of ramp to spare. The second half of the shipboard flight equation had been solved: An aircraft could also land on a ship.

History's *second* shipboard takeoff was not long in coming. In less than an hour Ely took off from the same ramp. This time it was uneventful and he flew back to the Presidio. He was once more a press hero—for a little while. His daring caught up with him on October 9, 1911, when he was fatally injured in a crash while flying an exhibition at Macon, Georgia.

With the extravaganza of a three-ring circus, carrier aviation had been born. By 1912 there were even designs for aircraft steam catapults requested by the U.S. Navy. Overseas, Britain's Royal Navy had demonstrated it was possible to use the speed and direction of a carrier ship to aid in launching and landing aircraft. (Ely had flown only from ships laying at anchor.) By turning a ship into the wind, while underway during a takeoff, it was possible to combine the ship's speed and wind speed with that of the aircraft to obtain a fairly high true airspeed. Conversely, during landings, the speed difference between the aircraft and the ship's deck could be somewhat reduced; hence, slower and easier landings.

Some thirty years later the Grumman Wildcats and Hellcats were using basically these same launching and landing principles as they flew off the decks of the fast carriers in the South Pacific. What had been an exhibition of daring in Ely's day became routine (though admittedly at times a little nerve jangling) and thousands of successful carrier landings and takeoffs were accomplished during World War II. Starting in 1930, Grumman Aircraft Engineering Company had quietly begun work that made that routine possible.

CONTENTS

GRUMMAN GENESIS

CHAPTER I

Short, stocky and pugnacious, the F4F Wildcat of the late thirties looked like a Navy fighter pilot's dream come true. A lot of the barrel-shaped lines of the trusty, but portly, F3F biplane fighters had been retained as a reminder that the aircraft was a Grumman. Even the chain-driven retractable gear still cranked up into the forward fuselage flanks. At a time when nearly everyone else was dreaming of sleek inline-engine fighters for the USAAC—the P-38, P-39, P-40, and in Europe they had the Spitfire, Hurricane and Me-109—the U.S. Navy was standing pat with the reliable air-cooled radial engines that had served so well in its aircraft throughout the thirties. The Navy was not about to have one of its pilots go down in the drink, miles from anywhere, just because a stray bullet punctured the engine's glycol system. The main difference with the Wildcat was its short midwing monoplane arrangement in place of the yellow fabric-covered bi-wings of the predecessor F3F's.

The scrappy little F4F's origin goes back to the day of Eugene Ely's first shipboard landing and takeoff. While the public was amazed at his stunt, official Navy interest was limited at best. The British Royal Navy, however, did test a couple of flights on May 4, 1912, from a ramp on the HMS *Hibernia*. Being the preeminent naval power in the world in those days the British were always ready to try new ideas. The flights were performed by Cdr. Samson and Lt. Malone while the vessel was underway. A few people in the Admiralty liked the idea of using shipborne aircraft for reconnaissance and fire control in conjunction with the big gun battleships and cruisers. However, they did not want useless aircraft-handling paraphernalia present on the decks of capital ships during an engagement. Seaplanes might have been one way of handling the situation but they were flimsy at best and hard to handle or retrieve in the rough open ocean. The other option, following the lead of Ely, was to build a flight deck on a ship that could be used exclusively to transport, launch and retrieve aircraft at sea.

The Cunard liner *Campania* was soon fitted with a 230-foot-long deck—from which seaplanes were only *launched!* Oh well, it was better than lifting them over the side with a crane—that is how they were retrieved! The next step was to mount a 200-foot land-plane flight deck on the HMS *Furious*. On August 2, 1917, the *Furious* became known for seaborne aviation's first pilot casualty. Squadron Commander E. H. Dunning, after making a successful landing on its deck, took off and tried once more. He and his Sopwith Pup went over the side, and he was drowned when a tire blew on touchdown. After the accident, arresting gear similar to that Ely had used was installed. However, the sudden stops wreaked havoc on the flimsy aircraft's longevity. About three landings with the system and an airplane was ready for the boneyard.

The first of 54 production F3F-1 fighters built in 1936. BuAer Number 0211 was delivered to the Navy at NAS Anacostia by race and test pilot Lee Gehlbach on January 29, 1936. (Grumman)

A parallel development effort was to tow a barge behind a ship traveling full steam into the wind. By means of a quick-release device, a Sopwith Camel mounted on the barge could be brought up to takeoff speed, released and then flown away. The system was unwieldy but on one occasion a Zepplin was shot down over the North Sea by one of the barge-based Camels. A number of different aircraft types were tried with the barge technique, but the complex system fell by the wayside.

By now, however, many landings were being made on the same decks from which planes were launched, by using the new arresting gear and cables. After fitting a few more ships with temporary decks, the British finally completed what is considered the world's first true aircraft carrier, in September 1918, two months before World War I ended. The superstructure amidship was eliminated on the HMS *Argus* and the whole length of the ship became a flight deck. She could accommodate twenty aircraft in her hangars. She could also make 21 knots which, when combined with wind speed, made landings and takeoffs relatively easy.

With the war over, the United States also took a serious look at carrier aviation by converting the collier *Jupiter* into its first carrier, the USS *Langley*. Japan, also a great naval power, began from scratch rather than revamping an existing ship, and built the *Hosho* as a carrier from the keel up. While the *Hosho* and *Langley* never met, they were the vanguard for a new type of warfare that, in another two decades, would explode into the deadly carrier battles of Midway and the Coral Sea.

The *Langley* entered operational service in 1925, after three years of trials. She carried thirty-four aircraft and many a naval pilot learned the art of carrier flying while serving aboard her. Outmoded by 1937, she was converted to a seaplane tender and, as such, was sunk early in World War II.

By December 1941 the United States had seven carriers in operation. Their names and dates of commission were as follows: *Saratoga*,

November 16, 1927; *Lexington*, December 14, 1927; *Ranger*, June 4, 1934; *Yorktown*, September 20, 1937; *Enterprise*, May 12, 1938; *Wasp*, April 25, 1940; and *Hornet*, October 20, 1941.

During the same time frame Great Britain, France and Japan had also built up their carrier aviation capabilities. In 1939, the international carrier scorecard looked like this: Great Britain, seven commissioned, six under construction; Japan, six commissioned, two under construction; France, one built, one under construction; and even Germany had one under construction. Hence, at the war's beginning, there were quite a few aircraft carriers in the world equipped with hundreds of fighters, dive bombers and torpedo bombers—all ready for conflict.

In the early days of carrier aviation the planes were light, even kitelike with low landing speeds. But it soon became obvious that the old sandbag-and-rope method wasn't going to work with the heavier, faster aircraft of the late twenties and early thirties. A new system was developed; however, it still worked on the same principle. The arresting cables strung across the deck were now wrapped around drums for easy re-tightening and the energy absorbed in stopping a plane was accommodated by a hydraulic accumulator system.

The system worked well and had the ability to be quickly returned to a retrieval position. It made it possible to land aircraft at a fairly rapid rate. That was important for, after a multiplane mission, the return to the carrier had to be accomplished with some haste, since the aircraft would be running low on fuel. Rapid aircraft retrieval also allowed a carrier more time to perform evasive maneuvers in a combat situation rather than hold a steady course into the wind during prolonged landing operations.

Along with the development of uncluttered carrier decks, service elevators to raise and lower aircraft to hangar decks below, and the all-important arresting gear that made the whole sequence possible, there was the development of the carrier fighter itself. Due to the nature of carrier operations the aircraft, while appearing to be about the same as land-based machines, included many subtle differences.

The retractable tail hook was a good case in point. The hook had to be strong enough to stop the careening weight of the aircraft when it grabbed the arresting wires strung across a carrier's deck. This meant its attachment to the aircraft's aft end had to be sturdy, with the whole rear fuselage beefed up to absorb heavy loads in an area that land-based planes did not need to be concerned with. The hook had to be retractable so as to not be in the way during land-based operations, and also to fulfill general streamlining requirements.

Due to the sometimes violent stop, when an airborne plane's hook grabbed the arresting cables, the landing gear had to absorb substantial punishment when the aircraft slammed onto the deck. Therefore, landing gears had to be much stronger than would normally be required of a land plane.

Another unique item, particularly after the introduction of monoplane shipboard aircraft, was the folding wing. By folding the wings, many more aircraft could be transported aboard the carrier, both on and below deck.

Reliability of the engine, even when suffering battle damage, was of extreme importance, for there were no emergency landing fields at sea. Therefore, the relatively simple tried-and-true radial engine was used almost exclusively by the U.S. Navy to power its combat aircraft. The thought probably was, if it was good enough for Lindbergh, it was good enough for them.

Additional radio equipment was also required, along with better navigational gear, so that the aircraft could find its way back to that pinpoint in the ocean, the carrier, which might be many miles from where it was when the aircraft took off on its mission.

In general, then, carrier aircraft did not have quite the performance of their land-based brethren. This was due to the comparatively unstreamlined radial engines, heavier landing gear, arresting system and the extra weight attributed to the wing-folding mechanism, radio and navigational equipment. Last, but not least, the fuel capacity often had to be greater to accomplish long over-water missions.

Another difference from land-based operations, vital to successful carrier operations, was the LSO—Landing Signals Officer. He was the maestro who joined pilot, aircraft and carrier deck in a thrill-a-minute act that controlled all final landing movements. His presence ensured that the aircraft landing attitude coincided with the carrier's pitching deck. This was important, considering that many Navy pilots will tell you a carrier landing in a rolling sea is little more than a controlled crash. The LSO stood at deck level, aft, near the port side of the carrier. In each hand he held brightly colored paddles that made his arm positions readily visible to the pilot lining up his final approach to the carrier deck with preset speed and power. The LSO usually knew the pilots and their idiosyncrasies, and with computer speed was able to make adaptations to help them make safe landings on a lurching deck; even at night, by using lighted paddles.

The hand-paddle signals consisted of eight positions: Arms outstretched wide meant everything was ok. Both paddles held low to the LSO's right meant the arrester hook was not down, an item of grave consequence. The paddles at chest level meant to speed up; the LSO's left arm extended meant the plane was coming in too fast. One paddle held low on both sides meant the plane was coming in too low and a little altitude was needed. A cut across the throat with a paddle meant the pilot should cut his engine and set down (the most welcome signal the pilot could get).

The final two signals were: Paddles outstretched and in a bank to right or left conveyed to the pilot to perform the same maneuver, that is, bank right or left to avoid bounding on the deck. If there were problems at the last minute, the LSO would hold the paddles cross-armed above his head and wave them. That was a waveoff and the pilot was expected to ram the power to full throttle and get the hell out of there—He was not about to make a successful controlled crash, just a *crash*.

Lest it be thought that LSO's never saw aerial combat it must be mentioned that the Navy's highest ranking ace of World War II had performed the duties of an LSO. That was Lt. Cdr. David McCampbell, whose story will be told in a later chapter.

A brief review of carrier planes leading up to the Grummans includes some rather interesting aircraft. The first official USN aircraft to make a carrier landing was an Aeromarine 39-B. The event occurred on October 26, 1922, aboard the new and still uncommissioned USS *Langley*. The first decent aircraft for carrier use came along in 1926, the Curtiss F6C-2, which was the beginning of the line of Curtiss fighters that culminated in the famous Hawks. By 1927 the Boeing F3-5 had also appeared. It too was a biplane and it was to eventually evolve into the equally famous F4B-1 in 1929. Vought came out with a two-seat observation plane about the same time, the OU-1. Between the Voughts, Curtisses and Boeings, the planes evolved through a progression of models, each better than the previous.

However, to be honest, those early Navy fighters were a somewhat ragtag bunch of flying machines when compared with their land-based cousins. Due to a lack of funds, development work came to a standstill through the late twenties and into early 1931. The existing aircraft were slow and sterile designs and were used long past the date of their obsolescence. The same circumstances held true with most other countries—carriers were ready to go but with no really good aircraft to put on them.

The British efforts during the same time period were, of course, much the same. Their most unusual contributions were the names of some of their planes, Sopwith Cuckoo, Fairey Flycatcher and Nieuport Nightjar, all staid biplanes. Japan was also in the same dreary rut with the Nakajima A1N1, a licensed version of the Gloster Gamecock. In 1931 the Japanese did introduce, however, the Nakajima A2N, a native-designed biplane fighter every bit as good as those of the Western world. Each country was hoping to make the carrier work and each was attacking the problem in the same manner with similar results.

The Grumman Aircraft Engineering Company was founded December 6, 1929, shortly after the October 29 stock market crash. That took real optimism. Premises for the new firm opened for business in January 1930, at Baldwin, Long Island, New York. That was followed by several subsequent moves from time to time during the early thirties with the firm finally locating (since 1936) at Bethpage, Long Island, New York. It was to be a successful business venture and its stock has paid a dividend every year since 1933.

The new airplane company was aggressive. With its design entry into the business it soon established a firm Navy/Grumman relationship. Even now, if it's a first-line U.S. Navy fighter the chances are pretty good it's a Grumman.

Spearheading the new operation was LeRoy R. (Randle) Grumman, an engineering graduate of both Cornell and MIT, a World War I naval aviator and, more recently, a test pilot and plant manager with the Loening Aeronautical Engineering Company. Loening had produced its famous amphibian scout planes for the U.S. Army and Navy between 1923 and 1928. They featured a chain-driven retractable landing gear that swung up to either side of a large center float. The gear was partially the invention and handiwork of LeRoy Grumman. Along the way Loening had also picked up two other individuals who would figure in Grumman's future. They were Jake Swirbul, Loening's shop and production manager, and Bill Schwendler, a top NYU aeronautical engineering graduate. The Loening Company was merged with Keystone Aircraft in the late twenties. That combination was then soon absorbed by the Curtiss-Wright Corporation.

Grumman, Swirbul and Schwendler left during the volatile takeover to form a corporation to service and overhaul Loening amphibians for the Navy. These low-key beginnings were to culminate with high public praise for the company's products in World War II. Admiral John S. McCain, commander of carrier task force 38, told a conference of labor leaders in Washington, ". . . the name Grumman on a plane or a part has the same meaning to the Navy that 'Sterling' on silver has to you." Today it still holds true. There has never been a bad production Grumman aircraft. In fact, the company's products have been so tough the firm has acquired the nickname of "the Grumman Iron Works" through the years. And during World War II it won five of the coveted Navy E awards for excellence.

Once founded, it wasn't long before Grumman's Loening repair business evolved into manufacturing as well. By the end of 1930 the new company had designed and produced eight large amphibian floats for the Navy after landing an initial order for two prototypes. It was confident of its new prototypes, for both Grumman and Swirbul rode along as observers during the first catapult launch test. The retractable-geared floats were used to modify Navy 02U and 03U land-based aircraft into seaplanes for use off cruiser and battleship catapults. With the chain-driven retract

One of 81 production F3F-2's built during 1937–38 for the U.S. Navy and Marines, the first being delivered in July 1937. It was a colorfully painted aircraft and for a time, starting in July 1938, it equipped all Navy and Marine fighter squadrons. (Grumman)

wheels the converted aircraft were still capable of use on airfields and aircraft carriers.

The Vought 02U-4 Corsairs, for example, were mounted on the Grumman floats with a sturdy system of streamlined tubing and cross cables. The floats were twenty-two feet ten inches long and four feet two inches wide when the wheels were retracted. They were fitted with a retractable tail hook for carrier landings. The floats worked well and between 1931 and 1932 Grumman built another fifteen units of an improved design.

By now Grumman had also built its first aircraft, a fighter plane. It was the two-place XFF-1. Since the company had a lot of experience with retracting landing gears it made this a feature of its new biplane, pulling the wheels up along the fuselage sides right behind the engine's firewall. The idea for the new fighter had come about when the Navy asked Grumman to design a retract gear for its then-current Boeing fixed-geared fighters. Grumman quickly saw that it would take a great deal of redesign of the Boeing aircraft to be able to accept it—so the company just proposed designing a whole new fighter plane instead. On March 28, 1931, the Navy agreed to the project and provided a contract for a prototype. The retract gear was a new item for any fighter in the world designed for production. The gear helped give the novel aircraft a top speed of 201 miles per hour, over 20 miles per hour faster than other fighters in the service, and this was a *two-place* configuration. The aircraft, popularly known as *FiFi*, first flew December 29, 1931. Flight testing included one unfortunate wheels-up landing but neither the Navy pilot nor the aircraft was seriously hurt. The Navy had twenty-seven of them built during 1933. Thus began a series of biplane fighters, all with side retract gear, that was to become a Grumman trademark. It wasn't until the much later World War II F6F Hellcat that Grumman finally adopted a more conventional method of landing-gear retraction.

The ensuing biplane fighter series were bought in relatively large numbers by the Navy to outfit its new carriers: fifty-four F2F-1's, fifty-four F3F-1's, eighty F3F-2's and twenty-seven F3F-3's. They were indeed most colorful birds with chrome yellow wings and red, green, blue or white tails and engine cowlings. The tail and cowl colors denoted the craft's squadron or carrier.

The Grumman biplane series almost continued into the F4F. F4F biplanes? Every aviation buff knows that the F4F was the famous Wildcat, with a monoplane layout. Well, it almost wasn't. In 1935 those F3F biplane fighters, the colorful ones just mentioned, were the lifeblood of

Grumman and were very much in vogue with the U.S. Navy. The Navy issued a competition document for a new carrier fighter in November 1935. Since everything had gone well so far for Grumman's great biplane designs why not refine the design still more and continue the winning string of fine naval biplane fighters?

Grumman engineering design number 16 was to be an improved F3F-1. It was to have shorter, equal span wings of twenty-seven feet rather than the thirty-two-foot top span of the F3F-1. It was hoped this change might increase the aircraft's speed to some degree and make it more compact for carrier use. Grumman performed the aero engineering and design work necessary to make a proposal and on March 2, 1936, the Navy Bureau of Aeronautics awarded the company a contract to go ahead with the detail design and construction of a prototype. All through that spring the prototype moved along under the direction of Chief Designer William Schwendler. It looked as if a fourth version of the tubby Grumman biplanes might go into production.

However, before long, the Grumman F3F-2, an improved version of the F3F-1, came out fitted with a Wright Cyclone engine. Unfortunately (or fortunately) its performance with the jacked-up horsepower nearly equaled that of the projected F4F-1. That was bad enough but there was yet another more ominous factor for the new biplane design. There was a new kid on the block: Brewster Aeronautical Company. Brewster was, overnight it seemed, designing a fighter that would knock the socks off anything that Grumman had ever imagined: the XF2A-1. Compared to it, Grumman's F4F-1 design looked antiquated, as it truly was. And the Grumman project had not even left the drawing board yet! The Navy was also aware that its fighter designs were getting way behind those of the land-based fighters under development. With agreement from all, the Grumman XF4F-1 design was terminated.

In June 1936, Brewster Aeronautical Company received a development contract for its new monoplane fighter. On paper the Brewster looked terrific and light years ahead of anyone else's design. Prepared by Brewster designers Dayton T. Brown and R. D. MacCart, the craft was of midwing monoplane design with a span of thirty-five feet. Its very bulbous fuselage had a length of twenty-six feet 4.9 inches. It featured wing-mounted retractable landing gear. In many respects it was almost as close a design to the old Gee Bee R-1 racer as any production aircraft ever came—a Gee Bee with a retractable landing gear. It was quite fast too, with an estimated maximum speed of 321 miles per hour.

Five hundred seven of the craft were built before the last one came off the Brewster line in March 1942. Why March 1942? That was right when we needed all the fighters we could get our hands on. Well, it turned out, in spite of its fancy design, the plane wasn't worth a damn as a combat machine. The Japanese Zeros, much more maneuverable, made absolute shreds of the Buffalos at Midway. The F2A landing gears were as apt to collapse as not during a hard carrier landing. The U.S. Navy gave the F2A's to U.S. Allies: Dutch, English, Australians and New Zealanders. Any plane was better than none at all! They didn't like them much either and as soon as they could be replaced with better equipment the design quietly passed from the scene.

If the F2A served no other useful purpose, however, it got Grumman headed in the right direction toward a sturdy shipboard monoplane fighter that was more in keeping with what the rest of the world was doing. There was nothing wrong with the basic fuselage design, tail, engine or landing gear of the Grumman XF4F-1—it was just that those antiquated biplane wings had to go. On July 28, 1936, the Navy handed Grumman a contract for building a prototype of the new monoplane fighter.

Grumman continued to maintain the proven landing gear design with side fuselage retraction. A 1,050 horsepower Pratt & Whitney twin-row radial was chosen for the powerplant and it was predicted the new aircraft would be able to make about 290 miles per hour without much trouble. By the summer of 1937 the prototype was complete and ready for flight test. All the latest in aero-technology was there: all-metal semi-monocoque fuselage, wings and tail (except for the fabric-covered control surfaces). There was also a new NACA 23015 airfoil that provided a thick cross-section for the midwing which allowed for internal armament while retaining low drag characteristics. On September 2, 1937, the first XF4F-2 put air between its wheels and the runway, piloted by the careful experienced hands of test pilot Robert Hall. It performed well, as expected. However, getting from the XF4F-2 to the production F4F-3 Wildcat was one hell of a tussle and will be detailed later.

The initial F4F-3's were not equipped with folding wings but the Navy desired that item. It would make deck handling and elevator use much easier. It would also make it possible to handle twice as many fighters aboard its carriers. A contract change was made during early 1939 to make the wings fold on all subsequent F4F-3 aircraft to be delivered. Grumman came up with an engineering solution for the requirement, some say by an engineer experimenting with a paper clip and a pencil eraser.

The skewed-axis folding-wing version became the F4F-4 and, on the first aircraft, the wings were folded hydraulically. It was soon decided, however, to go to a manual system to save the weight and space of the hydraulic folding mechanism. The new manual system worked well and, when folded, the wingspan was reduced to only fourteen feet four inches. The XF4F-4 first flew in April 1941. Now that the flying characteristics, as well as the ground handling problems, were well under control the Navy/Grumman relationship continued once more solid as a rock. Working together, in fact growing up together, Grumman and the Navy Bureau of Aeronautics were well on their way to transforming the Navy into a modern, mobile, hard-hitting fighting force.

Grumman felt pretty good about its new fighter and gave some thought to trying the Wildcat on a nonstop cross-country run that would break Howard Hughes' January 1937 record. A closer look by cooler heads pointed out that if they did break the record it would be by damned little and if they didn't—well, at minimum it would be bad press. That was the end of that.

The French had a couple of new carriers in the making (the *Joffre* and *Painlevé*) and since the Germans were starting to growl at their doorstep they were quickly interested in filling those new flight decks with Wildcats. A fly in the ointment was the engine. The Pratt & Whitney works was inundated with orders for U.S. warplane engines and it was unable to increase production to fulfill the French requirements. There was a solution, though: Curtiss-Wright was standing by with its R-1820-G205A Cyclone powerplant. The French agreed to place an order for 100 of the new 1,000 horsepower Wright-engined Wildcats. The aircraft's Grumman designation was G-36A instead of the G-36 nomenclature for the American planes.

Unfortunately, Germany invaded France in May 1940 just as flight tests were commencing on France's G-36A's. The whole deal, of course, went down the tubes when the French defenses were penetrated in June. The British, now also with their backs to the wall, took over the new fighter order on July 27, 1940, and called them Martlet I's—even before the U.S. Navy had received *its* first F4F-3's!

The U.S. Navy probably didn't mind, for the two-stage supercharged Pratt & Whitneys on *its* prototype planes were not functioning too

Perfectly balanced at the center of gravity, the prototype XF4F-2 is hung by a chain with landing gear retracted to prove the point. Its first flight was September 2, 1937. Fuselage and tail lines were quite similar to the never-built XF4F-1 biplane design. (Grumman)

well. In fact, even the Wright engines were beginning to look pretty good. Therefore, a new model Wright-powered Wildcat was created. The XF4F-5, powered by the Wright R-1820-40, proved out well in the summer of 1940. The Navy elected to go with it for a time and two prototypes were completed. Meanwhile, Pratt & Whitney, aware of the competition, managed to fix its problems. The Navy then elected to revert to the original Pratt & Whitney R-1830-70.

By the end of 1940 the Grumman order department had logged requests for 578 F4F-3's and F4F-6's, and the production people attempted to fill them. The first of the new F4F-3's were delivered to the Marines at Norfolk NAS as replacements for its F3F-2 biplanes. These early F4F-3's were delivered with chrome yellow wings, gray fuselages and brightly painted tail surfaces as had been standard on Grumman Navy fighters during the thirties. The original paint scheme was soon changed to all-sea-gray, the paint job of a combat airplane, in March 1941. Before long, one of the new F4F-3's was written off in an operational accident near the Anacostia Naval Air Station.

Some of the design details of the aircraft, in its early career, are of interest. The Grumman biplanes had taken care of the down-at-sea flotation problem by having wing-mounted air-inflated canvas bags as a part of their equipment. They generally worked well, the few times they were used. The bags, therefore, were carried over to the wings of the Grumman Wildcat. During a forced landing at sea they were to be deployed to keep the aircraft afloat until the pilot could be rescued. That was a great motive but on at least two occasions the bags inflated while the Wildcat was still in the air. What a lift killer! One incident was fatal. The only way the airborne inflated bag problem could be solved was by going into a dive, if there was enough altitude, and hoping the bags would rip off. There was another option, which the Navy considered and finally adopted: just get rid of the bags altogether.

Inside, that barrel-shaped fuselage had room for a cockpit and a half. It gave the pilot a certain amount of comfort not to be found in the cramped flight quarters of such inline-engined hotshots as the Spitfire and P-40. Another item of interest was the lack of any hydraulic system on the plane except for the wheel brakes. It was pretty simple compared to the elaborate hydraulic systems that were soon to be seen on other fighter designs coming off the drawing boards. Except for the flaps, which were operated by manifold vacuum, everything else was as mechanical as grandpa's alarm clock. Cowl flaps, trim tabs, control movements, arresting hook and, of course, landing gear retraction were all made up of simple mechanical movements well known for centuries—the screw, inclined plane, lever and wheel.

By 1940 this early production F4F-3 was a service test aircraft and, except for the spinner, was configured the same as the well-known Wildcats of World War II. Painted in Navy markings, the aircraft was a hit attraction when exhibited statically at the New York World's Fair in 1940. (Grumman)

Armament had been increased since the early XF4F-3. That had only a couple of paltry thirty-caliber machine guns installed in the nose cowl and another two fifties in the wings. The production F4F-3 menu called for four husky, fifty-caliber Brownings in the wings and later the number went up to six of these super lead-slingers. There was a tradeoff, though. More guns meant less room for ammunition. Therefore, on some aircraft the number was decreased to four guns with a lot more ammunition. Depending on the situation, either type of philosophy was the proper one. The guns were charged manually—how else with this mechanical marvel?

The engine was started with a cartridge starter that gave off a muffled explosion complete with smoke when the shotgun-sized starter shell was electrically fired. The propeller would turn over a few times and if the engine was suitably primed it would probably start. Once that chore was out of the way there was the good possibility of a flight. Despite not being able to see straight ahead during takeoff, the cockpit visibility wasn't all that bad. Of course, that was true of all tail-dragger fighter aircraft. It was one real good reason that tricycle landing gears came into being. With them, not only could the pilot see ahead during taxi, takeoff and landing, he could also fully apply the brakes without danger of a nose-over, thus avoiding damaging the prop blades and lower cowl.

Maneuverability while taxiing the Wildcat was not bad but the oleo shocks sometimes made it look harrowing. In a heavy crosswind they would collapse on the downwind side and the plane would roll (the wings considerably out of level), the upwind wing pointing toward the sky.

Takeoff, as with any high-powered tail-dragger, could give a moment of consternation to the pilot as he corrected for engine torque with brakes and rudder. If he didn't ground-loop during the takeoff run, the plane hopped off rather quickly and the pilot was treated to a very nice rate of climb. With the gear up, the Wildcat could move upstairs at about 5,000 feet per minute—at least until it passed 10,000 feet. Above that altitude the F4F-3 wasn't all that red-hot in the toss-and-turn department. Below 10,000, however, it could really rack up in tight turns, loop so the prop was chasing its tail, and slow roll as low as 80 knots.

The pilot had to keep his wits about him on touchdown to prevent a ground-loop, which would be caused by the narrow tread gear. While the landing run was less than 800 feet, a low oleo shock strut could make the dipping wing on that side seem as if it might touch the ground, with accompanying disaster.

The new fighter worked well and the first rigid-winged F4F-3 successfully completed its carrier qualification trials. It showed it could get off the short flight deck with great haste, only 283 feet with a seven-

This photo, taken in November 1942 aboard the auxiliary carrier USS *Santee* (ACV-29), shows the deck crew spreading and locking a Wildcat's wings. The F4F-4 was the first model Wildcat with folding wings and 1,168 were built during 1941–42. (U.S. Navy)

teen-mile-an-hour headwind. It could return for a landing on the carrier deck with a slow speed of only eighty-four miles per hour. Carrier life seemed suited to it. This was not surprising, for Grumman had been building successful carrier aircraft for nearly ten years and the Navy's peculiar design requirements were now routine for the Grumman engineers.

As the war continued, there were first one, then three rocket launchers mounted on each outer wing panel. The rockets were not used for aerial combat but, instead, on enemy ground targets, ships or landing craft. One other thing the Navy asked for and received was pilot armor plate and catapult launching gear mountings.

The Grumman G-36A, as mentioned earlier, was for European use and was originally designed with the Wright engine for sale to the French government. At the same time the British biplane Gloster Sea Gladiator, a naval version of the Gloster Gladiator of the RAF, was getting a little old. It was surely a very neat biplane fighter but was just no match for the Messerschmitt 109 the Germans were showing off to the consternation of the Allies. The Royal Navy needed something new. The G-36A's (or Martlet I's, as the British were to call them) had been manufactured and destined for the French Navy. But at the fall of that country, they were quickly taken over by the British. For thanks, one gave the British a Christmas present by shooting down a JU-88A over the Home Fleet base at Scapa Flow on Christmas Day, 1940. It was the first American plane in the hands of the British to shoot down an enemy. The Martlet I proved good enough that the British ordered 100 Martlet II's, which were Pratt & Whitney-powered F3F-3's (Grumman G-36B's). The first ten were fixed-winged; the remainder, of the folding-wing variety. By October 1940, eighty-one Martlets had been delivered to the Royal Navy. Some of the Martlets were assigned to the 802 Squadron aboard the converted German motor ship HMS *Audacity* to test the minicarrier idea. Two of them shot down a Focke-Wulfe Kondor early on in their careers.

In the North African desert campaign the standard British escort fighter was the twin-engined Bristol Blenheim, really not much of a fighter. They were somewhat antiquated for modern warfare. Here again, a more modern aircraft was needed. The British successfully threw in the

A Martlet I, of which 91 were built but only 81 were delivered. The other ten were lost at sea. While still in shipment to the conquered French they were taken over by the British, and assigned to the Royal Navy. (National Air & Space Museum)

Martlets to help back up the bomber forces in the western desert during the fighting of 1941. They were also used at Malta to protect valuable convoys making their way to that important stronghold. All in all, the fat, mid-winged fighter did well and was a credit to the Royal Navy in defending against the German and Italian offensives in the Mediterranean theater.

The early Wright-powered Martlets had two thirty-caliber guns in the fuselage nose and two fifties in the fixed wings. Once in operation the Fleet Air Arm quickly installed four fifties in the wings to get a little more muscle where it was needed.

During the same time frame Greece felt the thrust of Axis war efforts and, as a result, thirty F4F-3A Wildcats were diverted there in April 1940; but that country also fell to the Germans before delivery could be made. The Greece-bound Grummans had arrived at Gibraltar when the Greek resistance was overcome. The British, always ready for a bargain, took them over and shipped them off to the North African campaign as land-based members of the Royal Navy. They were dubbed Martlet III's and some were still operational in 1945. They eventually were to serve during the D-Day invasion and off the Norwegian coast harassing Germans.

In the United States, things had gotten more worrisome after the European war started. Thankfully, in 1938, the Expansion Act had suddenly allowed for purchase of 3,000 naval aircraft—and more carriers. Of course, Grumman was ready, and orders were easy to come by, if you had a first-class product like the Wildcat. A total of 185 F4F-3's and sixty-five F4F-4's were rapidly produced for U.S. Navy and Marine squadrons by Pearl Harbor day. Twelve of the new fighters had even been delivered to Wake Island on December 3, 1941, under the command of Maj. Paul A. Putnam and his sixty-man Marine air outfit.

During the December 7, 1941, Japanese attack, the new F4F-3's of VMF-211 at Ewa on Oahu were fired upon. Nine of the eleven in the military lineup were destroyed. None of the rest were able to get in the air during the attack. The Wildcat was no match for the Zero—Japanese lightweight terror of the Pacific. While the Wildcats were being destroyed on the ground in Hawaii (without firing a shot), the Japanese also totaled seven of eight Wildcats still on the ground at Wake.

TO BUILD A WILDCAT

CHAPTER II

The narrow-track landing gear, short bulbous fuselage behind the big radial engine and the squared-off wings and tail surfaces all gave the F4F the appearance of a mean machine. Loveliness of line, as found in the slender Spitfire or P-51 Mustang, was nowhere to be seen. That was all right, since Grumman was out to win a fighter plane contract, not a beauty contest. Closer inspection of the aircraft, however, tended to give the impression that it was a rather good-looking, first-rate aircraft after all.

This detailed description of the Wildcat will deal primarily with the General Motors-built FM-2 model which was produced in the largest quantity, 4,437 in all. The description will take a few side excursions to delve into some differences, such as engines and propellers, between it and other models.

The three-blade propeller was a Curtiss Electric constant-speed variety that was ten feet in diameter. Constant speed meant that the blade angle was automatically changed to allow the engine to put out maximum horsepower at all throttle settings—very handy during the high and low air speeds encountered during a snarly dogfight. The pitch settings went from a low of 18.5 degrees to a high of 53.5 degrees.

The constant-speed feature was under the control of the pilot by means of an electric selector switch and a governor push-pull control knob located on the left-hand side of the instrument panel. Engine rpm was increased by pushing the knob in and decreased by pulling the knob out. It *was* touchy and a small knob movement could result in a fairly large rpm change. Therefore, for small changes the knob could also be twisted, as a vernier, clockwise for rpm increase and counterclockwise for a decrease. The selector switch could cut out the constant-speed feature entirely and the propeller would then function as a *fixed* pitch unit. By toggling the switch right or left, any fixed pitch could be selected.

If for some reason the propeller electrical system became overloaded due to too much exercise, there was a circuit-breaker button also located on the propeller control unit that could be pushed in to reset the system. Other models of the Wildcat, such as the F4F-4, used Hamilton Standard constant-speed propellers that, on the bottom line, performed the same but were actuated hydraulically.

A Wright R-1820-56 Cyclone powered the FM-2. It was a single-row radial air-cooled nine-cylinder piece of machinery that, in the −56W water-injection model, could produce 1,350 horsepower at takeoff while turning up 2700 rpm. To help things along, the engine was fitted with an integral single-stage/two-speed supercharger. The cockpit control for the supercharger was a lever quadrant mounted on the left-hand side of the cockpit. It was pulled back for high blower and pushed forward for low

An early F4F-4 with red centered star and red-and-white-striped tail reaches for altitude. (Collect Air)

blower. As it was really a gear shift, it had to be all the way in one position or the other to avoid damaging the supercharger clutch. (Try driving a stick-shift car with the shift lever held between low and second and it is easy to see the reason for the warning.) Other cockpit engine controls were the throttle and mixture-control quadrant, also located on the left side of the cockpit, just forward of the supercharger quadrant; the carburetor air control on the left side of the instrument panel, as was the ignition switch; and the cowl flap control switch on the panel's right side.

On the pilot's distribution panel on the right side of the cockpit were the other engine instruments: the priming control system and the engine starter control. This last item fired the cartridge starter.

Unlike a modern electric-starting system, if all was not right with the engine priming, ignition and throttle settings, firing the cartridge produced nothing but a bang and another cartridge (about the size of a ten-gauge shotgun shell) would have to be loaded in the engine's starter breech by the plane captain. It could get real hot around the breech if three successive starts were attempted. Then everyone would have to wait for about five minutes for it to cool down so that another attempt at a start could be made. The cartridge, upon exploding, energized the starting mechanism, which in turn engaged the crankshaft with a sharp, but short-lived, spin up to starting speed. Eight Type C cartridges were normally carried in the engine accessory area in a box located on the engine-mount support tubing. The starter breech itself was located on the right-hand side of the engine-mount structure and was accessible through the right landing gear wheel well.

Before proceeding further, it should be noted that Pratt & Whitney series R-1830 engines were used on many of the Grumman-built Wildcats, most notably the R-1830-86 with a two-stage/two-speed supercharger. The Twin Wasp was a fourteen-cylinder twin-row radial air-cooled precision machine that produced 1,200 horsepower at takeoff and 1,000 horsepower at 19,000 feet. Primary use was on the Grumman F4F-4 model, of which 1,169 were built.

A powerful radial gulps fuel in pretty good quantities. The Wright engine in the General Motors FM-2 was designed to operate on AN-F-28 100/130 octane fuel, which was fed by, basically, a simple tank-pressure-feed system that included the possible use of two fifty-eight-gallon drop tanks, one under each wing, for extended range. The main tank held from 117 to 130 gallons depending on whether it was fitted with a rubber self-sealing liner. It was located in the fuselage under the cockpit. (On the Grumman F4F-3 there was also a twenty-eight-gallon auxiliary tank located behind the pilot.) The main tank provided a range for about 900 miles with that figure increasing to 1,310 miles with the use of the drop tanks. If drop tanks were used, fuel was drawn from first one, then the other, with the off-center weight of a full tank on one side and an empty one on the other being compensated for by the use of the trim tabs. Tank selection was by means of the four-position switch, as mentioned before. Its positions were: main tank, left droppable, right droppable and off (the latter for use during an engine fire or shutdown). The main tank was always used for takeoff and landing.

Fuel was carried to the carburetor by an engine-driven pump that was part of the engine accessory package. However, there was also an emergency electric fuel pump in the line for use in case of lowered fuel pressure at high altitudes, failure of the engine-driven pump, or during switching from one tank to the other. The electric pump switch was located on the left side of the instrument panel.

Keeping track of the fuel on board was by means of an electric fuel gauge located on the right side of the panel. The gauge measured only the amount of fuel in the main tank so the drop-tank fuel was measured by the pilot's guess and experience. However, there was a backup to the gauge in case the pilot got busy dogfighting and strafing the enemy. That was a warning light on the right-hand side of the instrument panel. It came on when only thirty gallons of fuel remained in the main tank—enough for thirty minutes flying time at cruise power.

Two items of interest concern the drop tanks. The first is the method of dropping them after the fuel was used, or before going into combat. This was done by sharply pulling two red (so the pilot could find them quickly) release rings, one on either side of the cockpit. Then the rings could be clipped back in their stowed position so as to not interfere with other controls.

The second item has to do with vapor return (actually, fuel return) to the tank. All engine fuel pumps push more fuel to the carburetor bowl than an engine can possibly use so that the engine is never at a loss for the vital liquid. The excess then goes back to the tank in the return line. The amount of fuel return could be as much as eight gallons per hour. It was therefore necessary to use up about fifteen gallons from the main tank before selecting a drop tank to make room for the return fuel. Otherwise, the fuel would be needlessly lost out the main tank vent line into the atmosphere.

An oil tank attached to the upper engine mounts held a nominal nine gallons, or eleven gallons with overload for long-range flights. It was distributed by an engine-driven oil pump and returned by scavenger pumps in the engine's nose sump and rear case. Engine oil in high-performance engines needed to be cooled, usually done by mounting some sort of radiator out in the fast-moving airstream. In the Wildcats' case the oil coolers were mounted on the inboard stub wings in stream-lined bumps on the wings' undersides.

One last item on engine-related fluids: The water-injection system carried a ten-minute supply of water. It was used for full combat power only under the direst of emergency conditions, for its usage could literally burn the engine up, or at least require a major overhaul. The water injection was introduced only after the throttle level was pushed past the detent limiting entry. That meant you *really* wanted it. The water prevented detonation (power-robbing ping in today's parlance) of the fuel in the cylinders at high-power settings.

The engine was mounted on the stainless steel firewall by means of a dynafocal mount, which was a collection of twelve steel tubes welded to the engine-mounting ring that attached to the engine. The tubes ex-

Grumman F4F Wildcat

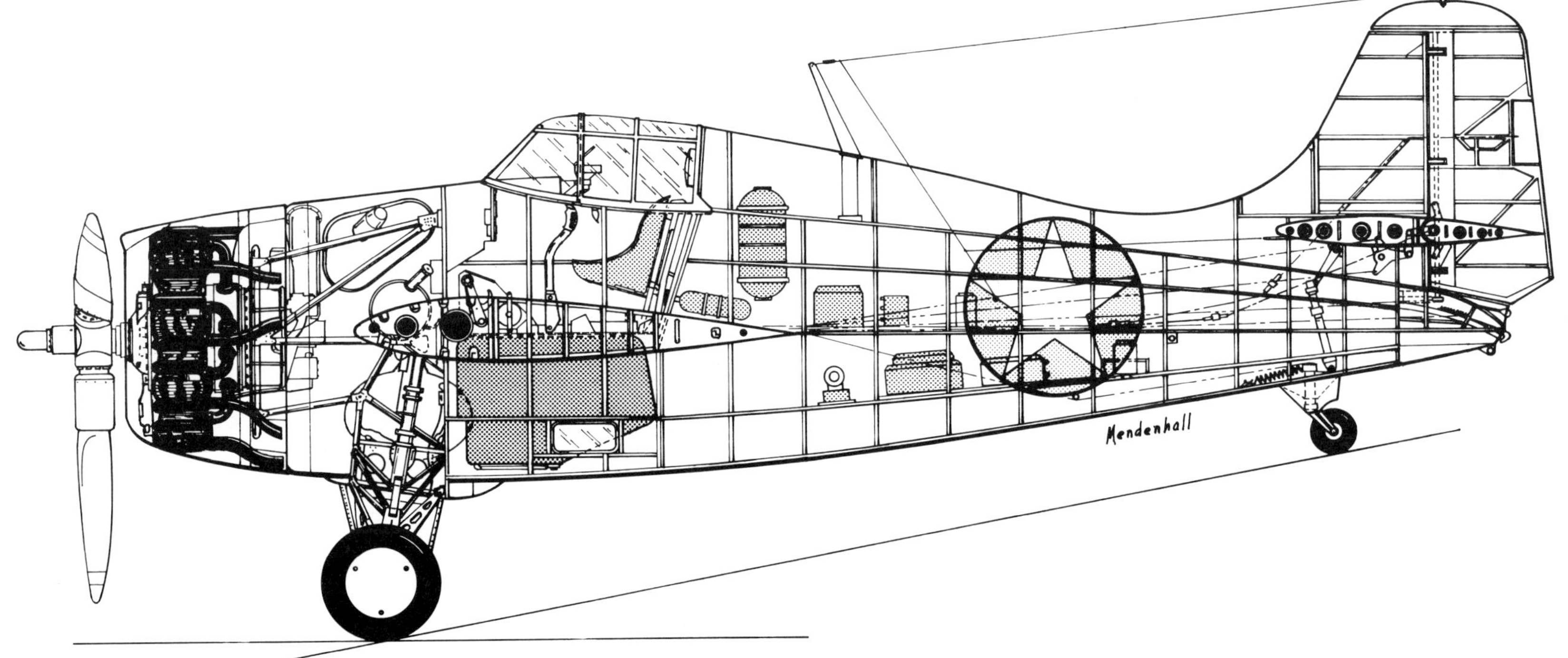

inboard profile

tended back to the firewall at precise angles where they were attached through antivibration rubber mounting pads. The engine mounts were long enough to have room for the oil tank, water injection tank and landing gear retraction mechanism.

Also in the Wildcat engine area was the engine cowl, designed not only to streamline the powerplant but also help in cooling by means of interior baffles and cockpit-operated cowl flaps located at the rear edge of the cowling. The cowl was removable by releasing flush-mounted fasteners so that the engine could be maintained and serviced, or even changed, easily.

The main landing gear retracted upward into the fuselage sides. This operation was performed manually by the pilot with a hand crank located on the right-side cockpit console. About twenty-eight turns of the crank raised the gear—and it had better be up before air speed built up too much, or the crank would turn so hard the pilot would put in a full day at hard labor just getting the wheels up. Of course, twenty-eight counterclockwise turns would lower it. (A quicker method of lowering the gear was to unlock it and pull a couple of g's in a tight turn or pullup. The crank would unwind rapidly—but God help you if you got a hand or arm in the way of the spinning crank!)

As the pilot cranked during retract, the aircraft sometimes took on a porpoising mode of flight as the control stick was moved slightly back and forth by the pilot's cranking motion. It could have been worse! The Russian Polikarpov required each main gear to be cranked up separately, which resulted in the aircraft rolling first one way and then the other, along with the porpoising.

The gear track was narrow, six feet five inches, making control on the ground difficult. However, it was sturdy, with 7.25 inches of total shock-absorbing deflection provided by low-pressure tires and the Bendix air/oil shock struts that were pumped up between 200 and 800 psi, depending on the aircraft's weight. Duo-servo hydraulic wheel brakes were activated by toe pressure on the upper part of the rudder pedals.

Coming from a long line of Grumman biplane Navy fighters, the retract mechanism harked all the way back to the Loening amphibian, for which LeRoy Grumman originally designed the gear. It consisted of a menagerie of gearboxes, sprockets, drive chains, hinge locks, counterbalance units, shock struts, drag links and other assorted mechanical paraphernalia to pull the wheels up against either side of the forward fuselage. The whole system was attached to the firewall and a lower fuselage-mounting beam—and it worked well! Actually, the Grumman landing gear was one of the main reasons the Wildcat's major competitor, the Brewster XF2A-1 Buffalo, fell by the wayside. The Buffalo's landing gear collapsed on a regular basis during carrier landings.

Completing the Wildcat landing gear was a swivel-type tail wheel with the tire pumped up to 175 psi for carrier use and 110 psi for land use. The wheel was locked in the straight-ahead position during airfield takeoff and landing and was allowed to swivel only to facilitate ground handling and taxiing. The wheel itself was a Bendix 10.5 × 4 × 4. It should also be mentioned that a hard-rubber, solid tire was used on the Grumman models during carrier operations.

Starting at the firewall, the fuselage was of semimonocoque construction. It was built of fourteen traverse bulkheads and circumferential rings used to define its cross-section. These were held in place by four corner longerons and six intermediate stringers that formed the side and top profiles. The longitudinal structure then provided the basic skeleton for the fuselage that was covered with conical Alclad sections, which overlapped at the section joints. The joints were sealed and flush riveted.

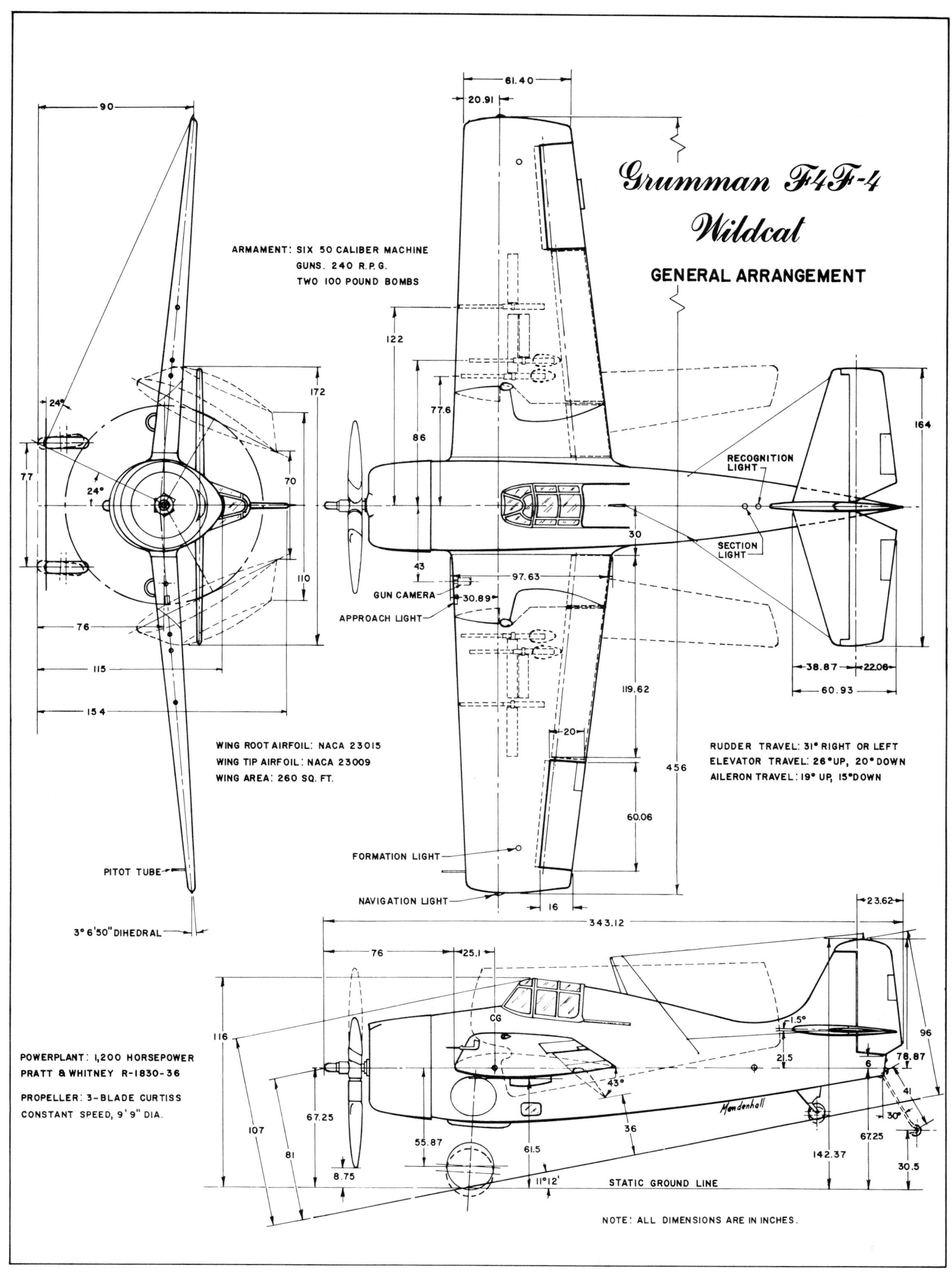

Grumman F4F-4
Wildcat
GENERAL ARRANGEMENT
ARMAMENT: SIX 50 CALIBER MACHINE
GUNS. 240 R.P.G.
TWO 100 POUND BOMBS
WING ROOT AIRFOIL: NACA 23015
WING TIP AIRFOIL: NACA 23009
WING AREA: 260 SQ. FT.
RUDDER TRAVEL: 31° RIGHT OR LEFT
ELEVATOR TRAVEL: 26° UP, 20° DOWN
AILERON TRAVEL: 19° UP, 15° DOWN
RECOGNITION LIGHT
SECTION LIGHT
GUN CAMERA
APPROACH LIGHT
FORMATION LIGHT
NAVIGATION LIGHT
PITOT TUBE
3° 6'50" DIHEDRAL
POWERPLANT: 1,200 HORSEPOWER
PRATT & WHITNEY R-1830-36
PROPELLER: 3-BLADE CURTISS
CONSTANT SPEED, 9'9" DIA.
CG
STATIC GROUND LINE
Mendenhall
NOTE: ALL DIMENSIONS ARE IN INCHES.

This construction made for an extremely rigid fuselage that was able to absorb large doses of combat punishment without failure.

The turtle-deck area behind the cockpit canopy was similar in construction, though lighter, and it faired into the vertical fin. The fin was also of monocoque construction consisting of seven ribs, the rudder post and a formed aluminum alloy covering.

The rudder consisted of an aluminum framework made up of nine ribs (eight for the F4F), a few cross-braces plus the all-metal adjustable trim tab. Right trim-tab travel was sixteen degrees twenty-one minutes and left tab travel was twenty-two degrees nineteen minutes to allow more travel on the side needed to combat engine torque during takeoff and carrier waveoff. The tab was connected to a control knob on the left cockpit console by means of a flexible cable and, even, a universal joint. The area of the fabric-covered rudder was about ten square feet, with a total vertical tail area being about twenty-four square feet on the FM-2. These areas were smaller on the F4F: 9.38 square feet for the rudder and 22.58 square feet for the entire vertical surface. The rudder was ball-bearing-hinged at three places on the rudder post and could swing thirty-one degrees left or right. The rudder was, of course, controlled through cables by means of the adjustable rudder pedals in the cockpit. Another vertical-tail feature was the asymmetrical airfoil that tended to "lift" the tail to the right to offset engine torque.

The horizontal tail spanned thirteen feet eight inches and was of similar structure as the vertical surfaces. The 30.43-square-foot stabilizer was of semimonocoque construction and the 18.62-square-foot elevator was fabric covered. The elevator could move twenty-six degrees upward and twenty degrees downward, the extra "up" travel being needed for flare during landings. Six ball-bearing hinges, three on either side, connected the elevators to the stabilizer. Trim tabs were on both elevators and could be operated from the cockpit—five degrees thirty minutes upward and fifteen degrees thirty minutes downward. The extra "down" travel was to compensate for the fuel load being used up during a flight.

The stabilizer was of single-spar construction with a torque tube connecting both elevators. Eighteen formed ribs of symmetrical section made up the rest of the stabilizer structure. The whole framework assembly was covered with flush-riveted, formed aluminum alloy sheeting. Each elevator was constructed of nine symmetrical ribs and the outline framework, including a wide, aluminum-alloy leading edge.

The spring-loaded tail hook was located in the aft end of the fuselage. This arresting gear was mounted on a track-guided carriage and controlled by the means of a cable to a slide control located on the left cockpit console. The hook transmitted arresting loads directly to the fuselage structure. An oleo strut and spring maintained force on the hook when it was locked in the extended position. An approach light on the instrument panel informed the pilot when the hook was down.

The rear fuselage behind the cockpit contained the pilot's oxygen tank, the wing flap vacuum tank, storage battery, radio installation, remote compass transmitter and dynamotor. The oxygen tank was part of a diluter-demand system. A pressure regulator on a bulkhead to the right and aft of the pilot was fitted with a pressure gauge at the intake port of the regulator to show the amount of oxygen left in the cylinder. The flowmeter was located on the instrument panel so that the pilot could monitor his oxygen supply. At high altitude without oxygen he could gradually become unconscious without realizing it. The oxygen cylinder held 514 cubic inches, which was enough for ten hours at 15,000 feet or five hours at 30,000 feet.

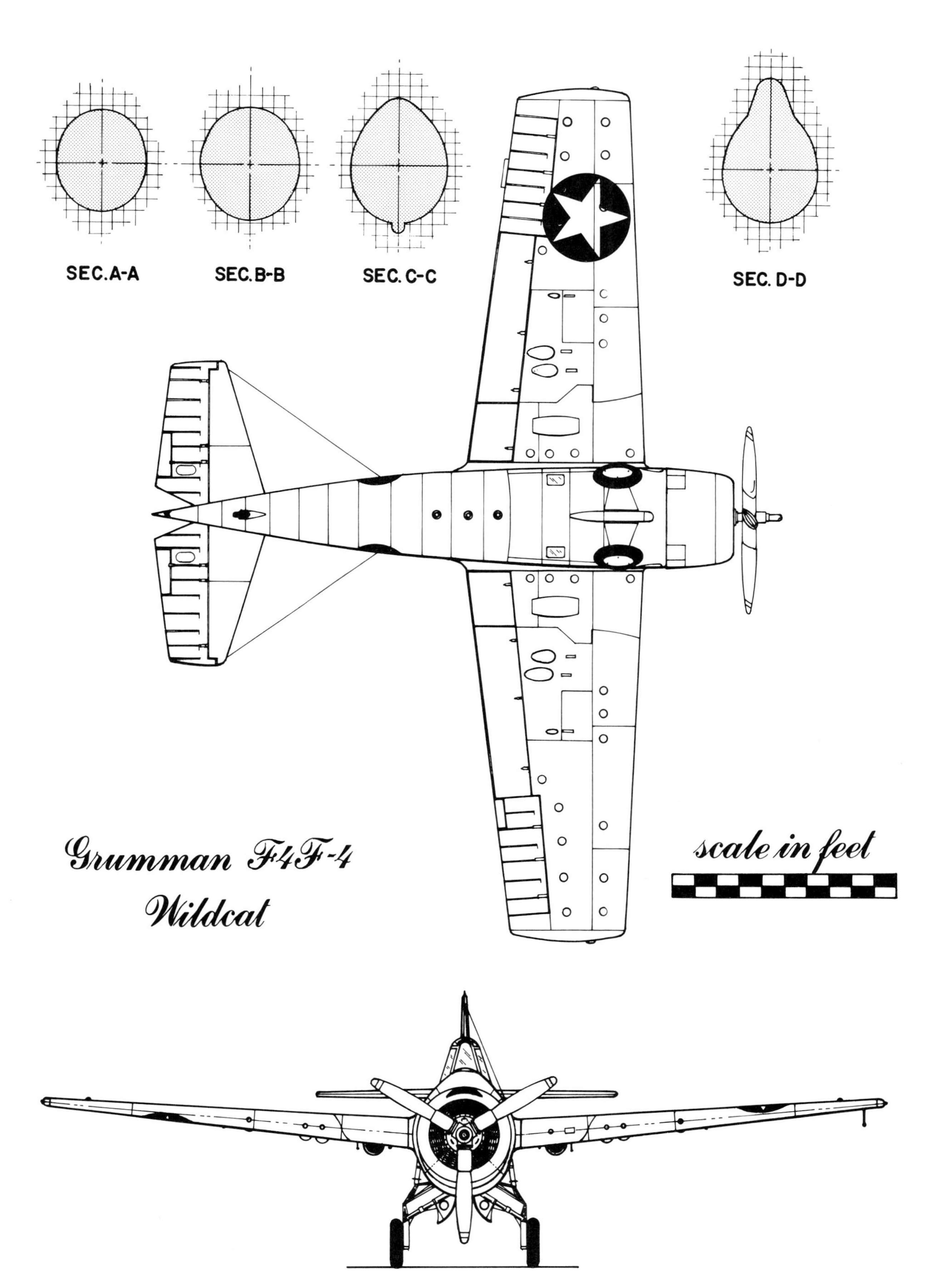
SEC. A-A
SEC. B-B
SEC. C-C
SEC. D-D
Grumman F4F-4
Wildcat
scale in feet

The flap vacuum tank and the operation of the flaps will be covered during the discussion of the aircraft's wing flaps. The 24-volt storage battery came into use primarily when the engine generator failed—such things as the radio and the electric propeller mechanism still had to operate, even though there was a failure elsewhere in the system.

The FM-2 aircraft was equipped with three different radio installations: AN/ARC-1 communication equipment, AN/ARR-2 navigation equipment and the BC1206 range receiver used for ferry and training operations. The radio controls for each were located aft of the pilot's distribution panel on the right-hand cockpit console. On later models the IFF (identification friend or foe) system was also installed. The dynamotor was an electric motor/generator unit that supplied the correct electrical voltage to the radio transmitter and receiver.

Also found in the aft-of-cockpit fuselage was a small baggage compartment (even pilots sometimes had to take their toothbrushes and a change of shirt and socks with them), with its door on the aft right fuselage side. Also, there was the radio mast internal mounting and, on some Wildcats, a stowed inflatable life raft in the turtle deck with an access opening on the right side.

The cockpit was enclosed by a bullet-resistant windshield capable of stopping thirty-caliber and, at a glancing angle, even fifty-caliber bullets. The windshield assembly consisted of two parallel panes of glass with an air space between them into which could be introduced hot air from the engine for defrosting. This system was activated by pulling a T-handle (located over the left rudder pedal) and rotating it clockwise to secure it in the outward position. The rest of the windshield assembly, held together by aluminum framing, consisted of three formed Plexiglas panels. A panoramic rearview mirror was located in the upper portion of that assembly. Two additional Plexiglas panes were located on either side of the lower fuselage so that the pilot could see downward.

The sliding canopy, also aluminum framed, consisted of six panes of Plexiglas and the assembly rolled rearward on a track attached to either fuselage side. For a pilot to gain entrance to the cockpit he climbed onto the wing walk by means of a step and a hand hole located on the rear fuselage side. A small door near the lower aft portion of the windshield was opened and the cockpit release handle inside pushed upward. The canopy could then be slid open. Due to the always present possibility of having to ditch in the ocean, both takeoff and landing were performed with the canopy open. Once airborne, the cockpit could be locked in any of four positions: full open, 5⅜ inches open, 1½ inches open, and closed.

For emergency canopy release, say, during a bailout, red-painted rings on either side of the forward canopy were grasped and pulled aft. This removed the canopy mount pins from the canopy track. With the pins pulled, a little nudge upward would send the canopy spinning off into the slipstream. Both rings had to be pulled at the same time. Pulling only one could jam the canopy, trapping the pilot, or cause the loose side to blow across the cockpit, possibly injuring him.

The cockpit consisted of right and left pilot consoles and the instrument panel. A few of the instruments and controls have been mentioned already. In addition, other main items were the pilot's seat, stick and the control pedals. The cockpit was armored front and rear with bulkheads that provided protection against fifty-caliber gunfire. A closer look will be taken of these items.

Across the top of the right cockpit side were a map case, a wiring diagram pocket and the arresting gear control handle. Below this, on the flat top of the console were, from front to rear: the recognition light switches, a permanently mounted check list, aileron tab control, rudder

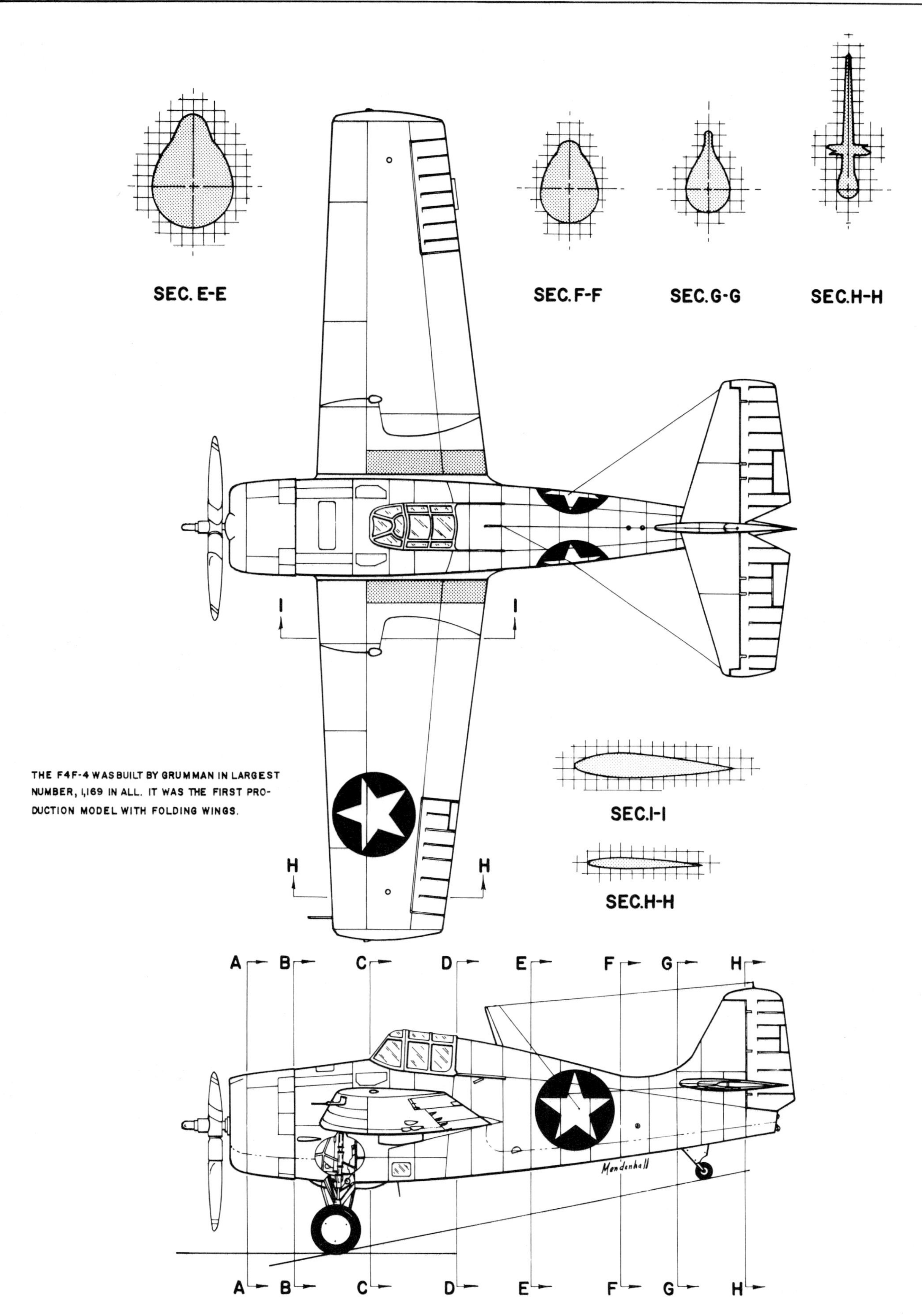
SEC. E-E
SEC. F-F
SEC. G-G
SEC. H-H
THE F4F-4 WAS BUILT BY GRUMMAN IN LARGEST NUMBER, 1,169 IN ALL. IT WAS THE FIRST PRODUCTION MODEL WITH FOLDING WINGS.
SEC. I-I
SEC. H-H
A B C D E F G H
Mendenhall
A B C D E F G H

Instrument panel of F4F Wildcat was given over primarily to flight and engine instruments. (Grumman)

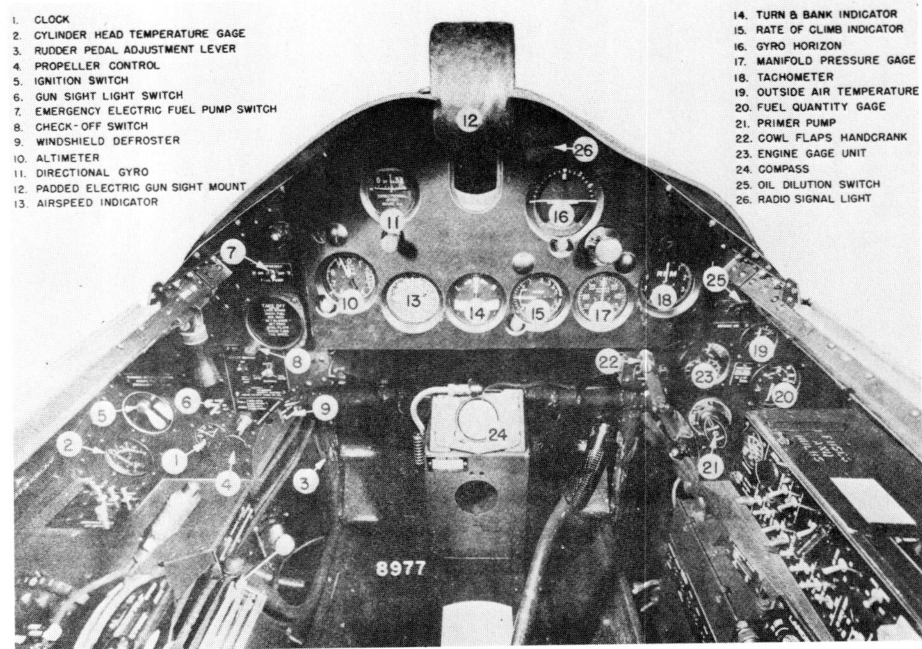

tab control, landing flap control crank and the fuel tank selector valve. On the console's side, next to the pilot's seat, were the tail-wheel lock control, throttle and mixture control quadrant, elevator tab crank, supercharger control quadrant and the droppable fuel tank release ring and mounting hook. Lower, alongside the seat, were the left-hand gun-charging handles. Also on this side of the cockpit were the oxygen controls and lip microphone switch.

The right cockpit console was somewhat more busy with the electrical and radio controls taking up much of the space.

On top of the console, toward the front, was the large cigar-box-shaped pilot distribution panel, a box containing a voltmeter, a power receptacle for electrical flying suits, and switches and knobs for such items as the master radio switch, section light, formation lights, wing running lights, tail running lights, gun selectors, gun camera (camera located in left wing root), pitot tube heater, starter, primer, battery, gun master switch, and rheostats for electric panel lights, chart-board light, cockpit light, compass light and instrument panel lights. Spare bulbs and fuses, as well as the active fuses, were located under the cover of the pilot distribution panel. Farther aft on the right cockpit console were mounted the IFF control box and selector switch, the communications equipment control unit, the navigation equipment control unit and the range receiver.

On the side wall of the console was the main junction box with the circuit-breaker reset buttons, the circuit-breaker box and reset buttons for rockets, and the landing-gear-position indicator. Next was the landing-gear hand-crank and lock, the generator cutout and the droppable fuel tank release handle for the right tank. Farther aft was the cockpit ventilator tube and the microphone/head-set jack box.

Along the right-hand side of the pilot's seat were, starting at the front, the pilot's seat-adjustment handle, right-hand gun-charging handles and the oxygen bottle shut-off valve mentioned before. On some Wildcat models there was also a landing-gear-positive-down indicator.

The left cockpit console in the F4F held the throttle and secondary controls of a mechanical nature. (Grumman)

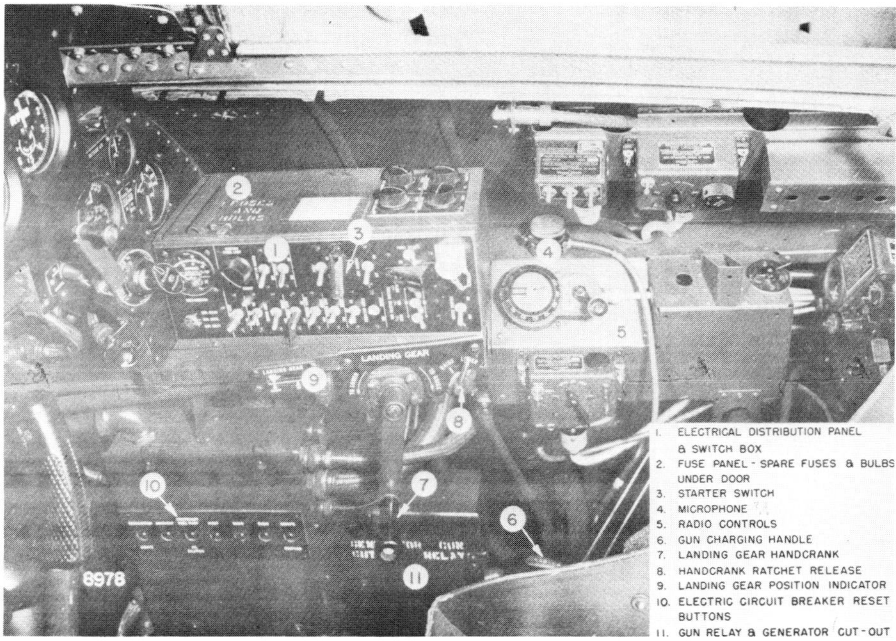

The right cockpit console in the F4F contained most of the electrical and radio gear. (Grumman)

The instrument panel was divided into four sections: the shock-mounted main panel, which contained the directional gyro, gyro horizon, altimeter, air-speed indicator, turn and bank indicator, climb indicator, manifold pressure gauge and tachometer; the right panel which contained the oxygen flow meter, the oil dilution switch, the cowl flap control crank and the engine gauge unit; the left control panel (starting at the top) held the emergency fuel pump switch, fuel quantity gauge, low-level-fuel warning light, gun-sight switch and rheostat, propeller selector switch and circuit breaker, carburetor air control, propeller governor control, ignition switch, clock and the cylinder head temperature gauge; and the lower instrument panel, which contained the compass, Mark III station distributor and the cabin air intake control. Between the lower panel and

The square tips on the Hamilton Standard propeller make this F4F somewhat unique. The interior of the folded outer wing panel is also plainly visible. (Collect Air)

the main instrument panel was the chart board that could be pulled out if desired.

The pilot's seat was adjustable to any of seven heights by pulling the seat lever and letting it settle (due to body weight) or raise (due to tension of the shock cords). Fore and aft adjustment was not needed, as the rudder pedals were adjustable. A shoulder harness and seat belt were also a part of the seat assembly, as was the adjustable headrest.

The control stick, of course, performed the normal elevator and aileron movements. The top of its hand grip contained the machine-gun electric trigger button. The rudder pedals, hinged to an overhead cross-bar, handled the rudder movement in the conventional manner and acted as brakes when depressed by the toes. The pedals were adjusted by pulling a release lever on the outside edge of each so that they would ratchet into one of four different positions. A Mark II reflector gun sight was mounted behind the windshield and above the instrument panel. One last cockpit item was the overturn structure behind the pilot's headrest, which protected him from being crushed in the event of rollover.

The wing of the Wildcat came in two varieties: folding and non-folding. The FM-2, as described here, had the folding variety. With a span of thirty-eight feet and an area of 260 square feet, the wing had a root chord of 8.135 feet that tapered to a tip chord of 5.117 feet. The trailing edge swept forward at about 7.5 degrees and the leading edge swept back at about 2.5 degrees. The airfoil section at the root was a NACA 23015, which tapered to a NACA 23009 at the tip. The wings were set at zero degrees angle of incidence. The ailerons' combined areas were 13.26 square feet, including the ground adjustable balance tab on the right wing and the cockpit adjustable tab on the left aileron. Aileron travel was nineteen degrees up and fifteen degrees down. Tab travel was plus or minus twenty degrees.

The wing flaps, of which there were four sections, could be deployed downward forty-three degrees. The combined flap area was 29.7 square feet. The wing was built in four sections: two stub sections from the fuselage to the wing fold line, and the outer panels to the tips. The structure of the stub wings consisted of upper and lower chrome-molybdenum steel channel beams, connected by a sheet aluminum web and a rear spanwise beam for strength. Four formed aluminum alloy ribs with aluminum stringers made up the airfoil shape. Aluminum alloy doublers (or reinforcing skins), plus upper and lower skins and a trailing-edge skin, completed the covering—all flush riveted together at the joints. At the fuselage/wing juncture a fillet smoothed out the airflow (and hid

This F4F-4, fitted with bomb shackles on the outer wings, is made ready for flight in 1942 by a group of Grumman technicians. (Collect Air)

the crack) between the two. Ten stringers plus the trailing edge were used for the spanwise structure.

Fittings for attachment of the stub wings to the fuselage were machined, high-strength steel forgings, as were the fittings for the outer-wing-panel attachment points. Each stub wing could support a fifty-eight-gallon drop tank, and the left stub provided a mount for the gun camera and an approach light. The leading edge of the right-wing stub mounted the inlet for the cockpit air-induction system. The streamlined engine-oil coolers were also mounted on the underside of each wing stub. On the stub wing's trailing edge were portions of the split flap.

The outer wing panels also contained sections of the aircraft's split flaps. They extended from the wing fold line to the ailerons. All four vacuum-activated sections of the flaps operated concurrently. The operating vacuum was supplied by the engine intake manifold and was either applied directly to the flap-actuating cylinders or stored in the vacuum tank in the fuselage behind the cockpit. The tank's capacity was such that it could operate the flaps to full deflection with the engine shut down.

Since engine manifold vacuum was still produced with the engine shut down—providing the propeller was windmilling—the actuating vacuum force was still more than enough to hold the flaps down against the airstream. In flight, as the engine power and rpm increased, the vacuum decreased and the flaps would retract under the airstream's push till they were retracted to about ten degrees at 140 knots (which was ok, as the plane was in the air and moving along nicely by this time). However, if the throttle was retarded, a high manifold vacuum would again occur and the flaps would return to their maximum forty-three-degree, full-down position. Of course, when at altitude they were subject to the vagaries of atmospheric pressure.

The outer flaps were made up of twelve formed aluminum ribs riveted to a thin trailing edge and reinforced at the joints with gussets. A stringer and torque tube added stiffness to the structure as well as the sheet aluminum undersurface and leading edge, which was flush riveted to the flap's skeleton structure. The flap top surfaces were left uncovered, as they served no aerodynamic purpose. The inner flaps on the stub wing were of similar construction except they were much shorter, only five ribs making up the structure. The outer and inner flaps were hinged in three places. All four flaps were actuated by vacuum cylinders and return springs. To help the pilot keep track of their positions, there was a small indicator affixed to the inner flaps.

Each aileron was mounted on three self-aligning, ball-bearing hinges inset in the formed sheet aluminum leading edges. Nine formed

An F4F-4, with canopy open, cruises above fleecy clouds. It was one of 1,169 of the folding-wing variants built. (Collect Air)

aluminum ribs were connected to the trailing edge with gussets and made up the structure along with a couple of diagonal ribs for added strength. The ailerons were fabric covered.

The outer panel layout consisted of nineteen formed aluminum ribs spaced ever closer together as their positions progressed outward toward the tips. The wing cross-section, or airfoil shape, was built in three sections about a forward canted spar of high-strength-steel upper and lower sections, joined with a solid aluminum web. Ahead of the spar were solid, formed aluminum leading-edge ribs. Behind the spar was a truss-work rib structure back to the rear spar. Behind that, more formed aluminum ribs were attached to the trailing edge with gussets. About ten channel-shaped stiffeners, or stringers, completed the framework, which was covered with formed aluminum alloy sheets that were flush riveted to the skeleton structure. The ribs at the fold line were nonwebbed and corrugated for stiffness.

The outer wing panels carried the aircraft's armament: four Browning M-2 air-cooled fifty-caliber aircraft-type machine guns on the FM-2, six on the F4F-3. They were fed from four (or six) ammunition boxes, the individual cartridges held together by a disintegrating metal link belt. The guns were secured to the wing gun mounts by quick-detachable trunnion bolt assemblies and mounting posts. Blast tubes surrounded the gun barrels to provide protection against the explosive forces on the wing's internal structure.

Gun heaters, in the form of electrical resistance wires connected directly to the generator, were located over the gun breeches and retracting slides. The guns were mechanically charged by means of handles on either side of the seat. Firing of the guns was accomplished by closing an electrical switch actuated by a button at the top of the control stick handgrip. That tripped an electrical solenoid on the guns' breech. The guns could be fired in salvo, or just the inner or outer two by means of a selector switch. For accuracy the guns were manually and optically bore sighted.

Another form of armament was the Mk-5 rockets, which were used for ground attack. On the FM-2 there were launchers for three rockets under each outer wing panel. There were two streamlined steel posts for each rocket: The forward post contained the fuse-arming mechanism and the rear post contained the electrical firing lead and a retarder to hold the rocket until it actually began firing. Firing was accomplished by selecting the rockets to be fired on the station distributor and pressing the electric firing button on top of the control stick. Instead of rockets, two 100-pound fragmentation bombs could also be carried on the outer launchers, one under each wing.

This General Motors FM-2 was one of 4,777 built, the largest number of any Wildcat variant. (Collect Air)

Each formed aluminum wingtip carried the running lights. Just inboard of the tip were the formation lights. The pitot tube was on the left wingtip. About halfway inboard on this same wing was the retractable landing light located on the wing's undersurface. In general, the Wildcats were painted either entirely gloss sea-blue or with sea-blue upper surfaces and nonspecular white undersurfaces.

Concluding the description of the aircraft, a few words about its characteristics and performance are needed. Some of the limitations and restrictions the pilot had to adhere to in flight were more concerned with whether or not the aircraft was carrying the two fifty-eight-gallon drop tanks. With one or more of the tanks, loops, snap rolls, chandelles, Immelmans and spins were not permitted. That pretty much canceled any chance of a dogfight with the tanks on. They were immediately dropped in the presence of the enemy.

Without the tanks, there were no standard maneuvers that the plane could not take. A few maneuvers could be performed with the tanks on such as wingovers, vertical turns, aileron rolls and inverted flight while entering a dive. There were no limiting air speeds during a dive and terminal velocity dives were acceptable—even with 100-pound bombs and drop tanks aboard. The flaps could be lowered at any speed under 150 miles per hour, above which the airstream would hold them up.

The landing gear also could be dropped at any speed except it was dangerous above 172 miles per hour. The air load on the gear could cause the cockpit handcrank to whip out of the pilot's hand and spin wildly, perhaps resulting in a broken forearm. What this actually tells us is that the Wildcat was one tough fighter aircraft with absolutely no restrictions on the pilot during combat—if he could take it, the airplane could!

A standard preflight check list included adjusting the shoulder harness and raising or lowering the seat to the desired level. A visual check of the red flags on either wing indicated whether the wing-fold locking pins were secured. The wings' folding or spreading was performed manually by ground crewmen. The wings were held in the spread position by the crank-operated locking pins. Cranks for the locking pins were located in the leading edges of the wing at the folding axis, behind hinged and latched access plates. The red flags mentioned earlier were a part of this mechanism. They retracted out of sight when the locking pins were secured. The folded wings were positioned along either side of the fuselage, held in place by jury struts between the wing tip and strut mount positions on the stabilizer leading edges.

Additional items of the preflight check list included checking out the cockpit for loose objects that could foul the controls, testing the arresting hook mechanism, the canopy release rings, rudder pedals and stick for freedom of movement. All instruments were uncaged, the clock wound and set, the battery switch turned on and the fuel gauge checked. Other items checked included oxygen system and gunsight operation, and that the Very pistol was loaded. Radio equipment was then checked out and a visual inspection for ammunition was made by the ground crewmen. At night, additional checks were made for proper operation of cockpit, section, formation, approach and recognition lights with the help of a ground crewman. With these preflight checks complete, engine startup was the next order of business.

With the ignition switch off, the throttle open and the mixture control in idle cut-off position, the engine was pulled through four or five revolutions by hand. This was to clear the lower cylinders of oil that might have collected, which could cause possible engine damage if not removed before startup.

The next steps were to fully open the cowl flaps, move the fuel selector valve to the main tank position and push the propeller circuit-breaker switch to ensure it was closed. The propeller selector switch was then snapped to automatic and the propeller governor control knob moved to full in for takeoff rpm. The supercharger control was then locked in the low blower position and the carburetor-air knob placed full in at the direct air position. The next step was for a crewman to insert an explosive cartridge in the starter breech. That was inside the cowl, and reached through the landing-gear wheel well opening. With the throttle set for 1000 rpm, the battery switch and emergency fuel pump on, the primer switch was closed for three to five seconds. That got a supply of fuel in the engine ready to burn when the engine was kicked over by the starter. With the ignition switch now turned to the "both mags" position, the starter switch was closed to fire the cartridge.

The engine started turning over with smoke and flames out the stacks and a groaning ragged rattle. The mixture control was advanced to auto-rich and, with flicking of the primer switch, that big radial Wright would smooth out to a throaty 1000 rpm rumble. And if it didn't start, the pilot pretty much began the process all over again. No question, it was a lot more difficult than starting the family chariot!

After warming up the engine with cowl flaps still full open and oil pressure checked, the carburetor-air T-handle was pushed full in and the throttle advanced to 1200 rpm. At that point engine operation, magneto operation, manifold pressure regulator, propeller and supercharger were checked, and the aircraft was ready for takeoff if all systems shaped up in a nominal manner.

The wing flags were once more checked to make sure they were down and out of sight. The tail wheel was locked, the canopy locked open, the aileron tab set at neutral, the elevator tabs set at neutral, the rudder tab set slightly to the right. The cowl flaps were rechecked to be open and the fuel switch checked for main tank position. Now the aircraft was about ready to roll. With the propeller governor control full in, the supercharger still set at low blower, the mixture control at auto-rich and the emergency fuel pump still on, the throttle was advanced to full throttle position and, with a last check of oil temperature, pressure and cylinder head temperature, the aircraft began to roll, lifting off at about 70 to 75 knots from a three-point position. As soon as the plane was safely airborne the gear was cranked up. The best climb speed was about 125 knots indicated and the cowl flaps and mixture control were tinkered with to maintain the proper cylinder head temperature.

Stalls, when the aircraft was clean (and with power), occurred fairly gently at about 68 knots, with the usual shudder occurring just

Three photos of the General Motors FM-2 version of the Wildcat. Note the higher rudder and fin that were added to increase effectiveness of controls against increased engine torque during waveoffs. (Collect Air)

before the nose dropped through. With the flaps in landing position the stall speed was reduced to 59 knots. During a high-speed terminal velocity dive the aircraft could reach a speed of about 370 knots at 15,000 feet and required a stick force of from 75 to 100 pounds to negotiate a pull-out. All other maneuvers were permissible except inverted flight, which was to be used only during entrance into a dive. That was because the fuel system was not intended to work upside down.

Landing the Wildcat was accomplished by first cranking the landing gear down and making sure the tail wheel was still locked. If a carrier landing was to be made, the tail wheel was *unlocked* and the arresting hook lowered. With the canopy now locked open, the carburetor air was pushed into the "direct air" position and the rpm were set for about 2100, with the throttle being retarded more as the altitude decreased. At that time the supercharger was also locked in the low-blower position and the cowl flaps opened a bit if needed. The mixture control was set at auto-rich. The flaps were lowered and an approach speed of about 85 knots was maintained until touchdown. In a crosswind, a steeper-than-normal descent was maintained. The tail wheel was set down first without any attempt made to hold the craft off for a more slow and gentle touchdown. That could allow the wind to get under the wings when the plane was in a vulnerable position.

One further characteristic that could cause a problem would occur in the event of a waveoff during a carrier landing. The pilot had to be prepared to apply forward stick pressure when suddenly applying full power, for that tended to raise the nose. If such was not done a stall could rapidly develop.

Once on the ground, or carrier deck, the engine was shut down using a nine-point check list that included idling at 800 to 1000 rpm until the cylinder head temperatures dropped to below 200°C. The engine was then run up to 1000 to 1200 rpm for one-half minute before shutdown.

There were a few emergency procedures to cover such things as fires and engine failures. The main remedies were to shut off fuel and electrical systems prior to landing. Water landings were with wheels up, flaps down and canopy open. The pilots manual assured the pilot there would be time to get out of the aircraft before it made its final plunge. It was a nice touch.

All in all, the Wildcat was a rugged bird and one that many a pilot truly believed in. While it could not take on the Zero in a dogfight, it could certainly protect the pilot with its rugged structure and good handling qualities. Built by the thousands it was still in production on V-J Day and still doing its job on the escort carriers sheltering the merchantman lifeline to the war fronts.

CHAPTER III — TAMING THE WILDCAT

There were at least fourteen distinct versions of the Wildcat during its production, from early prototype models to the final FM-2 built by General Motors. The prototype, the XF4F-2 (BuAer 0383), first flew September 2, 1937, a full three months before the competitive Brewster XF2A-1. The manufacturer's trials proceeded uneventfully, mostly flown by Bob Hall. The design was modified during this period to include changes in the cowling and the addition of a spinner to improve engine cooling. The aircraft was presented to the Navy on December 23 after being flown to Anacostia Naval Air Station. Testing and evaluation of the XF4F-2 comparing it to the Brewster XF2A-1 and the Seversky NF-1 (a seagoing P-35) got underway both at Anacostia and Dahlgren, Virginia. Things did not go well.

The Grumman's Pratt & Whitney suffered crankshaft bearing failures, causing long delays on the ground for repairs. Then the aft fuselage caught fire while in flight at 10,000 feet on February 14, 1938. The damage was repaired in a couple of days and by March 11 the aircraft had sixteen hours on it. The aircraft was transferred to the Naval Aircraft Factory on April 6, 1938, for deck-landing trials. Five days later, the engine quit as Navy Pilot Lt. Gurney made a simulated deck approach. The XF4F-2 flipped on its back damaging the landing gear, propeller, engine cowl, right wingtip and tail surfaces. The battered remains were shipped back to Grumman for repair. That was accomplished in about two weeks and the prototype was once more flown to Anacostia.

By the end of April, the Seversky competitor was out of the competition due to lack of speed and some stability problems in the lateral mode. The Navy, now digging hard to choose between the Brewster entry and the Grumman, put the XF4F-2 in the full-scale wind tunnel at Langley Field in May. While the top speed of the Grumman had proven to be a respectable 290 miles per hour at 10,000 feet, tunnel tests demonstrated that its speed might be increased by another thirty miles per hour with some judicious tweaking of the design. That would mean changing exhaust ductwork, smoothing out the contours of air intakes and gun fairings and, finally, adding covers over the wheel wells. Because of the problems on the prototype and the needed changes found in the wind tunnel test, Brewster won the fighter contract. On June 11, 1938, fifty-four Brewster F2A-1's were ordered.

But the Navy was still interested in the Grumman, for it had shown promise during the trials and there had certainly not been any basic flaws in the machine. In October 1938 it put up some money for the

The first XF4F-2 was flown September 2, 1937, by test pilot Robert L. Hall, winner of the 1931 Thompson Trophy Race in the stubby Gee Bee Model Z. He must have felt right at home in this chunky little fighter aircraft. (Grumman)

This three-quarter front view of the XF4F-2 shows off some interesting features such as the gunsight, carburetor air scoop, small propeller spinner, twin lower pilot visibility windows, rounded wingtips and, of course, the short pudgy fuselage. (Grumman)

development contract for the XF4F-3, an improved version of the XF4F-2. Meanwhile, Grumman had taken the XF4F-2 back to Bethpage. Now, with that contract in hand, it was dismantled till only the fuselage was left—the starting point for the new XF4F-3 model. The flying surfaces were totally modified to a new configuration with square wingtips and tail surfaces. The change of the wingtips, and an extension of the span from thirty-four to thirty-eight feet, increased the wing area from 232 square feet to 260 square feet and added substantially to the craft's dogfighting ability. That had to be done to bring the plane up to the standards that were being set by the Brewster XF2A-1 Buffalo.

The XF4F-2 had been powered by a Pratt & Whitney R-1830-36 that provided 900 horsepower at 12,000 feet. Now Grumman switched to a more powerful XR-1830-76 Twin Wasp, with a two-stage two-speed supercharger that belted out 1,050 horsepower at 11,000 feet. That would certainly help in the speed department—if it could be cooled. Accessing it

While still the same airframe (note the BuAer number 0383), the XF4F-2 had undergone numerous modifications to become the XF4F-3. Among them were the larger spinner, squared-off wingtips on a longer-span wing, and squared-off and reshaped tail surfaces. These changes made the aircraft look like a totally new design. (Grumman)

This right-side view shows the XF4F-3 aircraft as it was initially flown on February 12, 1939. It shows the aircraft on the opposite side from the previous photo. (Grumman)

for maintenance also presented some design problems; but, by late January 1939, satisfactory installation was completed. In the process, the overall length also was stretched from twenty-six feet five inches to twenty-eight feet. The rebuilt Grumman, now some 600 pounds heavier, took to the air for forty-five minutes on February 12, 1939, with test pilot Bob Hall at the controls.

On March 7, 1939, the Grumman fighter was once more flown to Anacostia for the Navy's evaluation. Over the next six months the aircraft was wrung out, modified, and then wrung out some more, as minor problems cropped up and were cured. During testing at Anacostia and Dahlgren, engine cooling was a real problem, particularly at high altitudes. Fixes for this included cowling flaps and spinner changes and the addition of cuffs to the propeller-blade shanks. The latter seemed to work the best.

Other modifications included an increased fin area, a reduced aileron area and a one-degree increase in wing dihedral. Additional development was done on the Grumman that included removal of the spinner during cooling trials. Many of these changes required the aircraft to be sent back to Bethpage with subsequent return to Anacostia. Finally, on May 15, 1939, the aircraft was flown to Anacostia by Navy pilot Lt. M.E.A. Gouin and on to the Naval Aircraft Factory in Philadelphia on the eighteenth.

Things at last were going pretty well for the Grumman offering. It went through some more tests at Langley's full-scale wind tunnel in De-

Cooling the XF4F-3 engine was a big problem with the large spinner in place and it was soon removed for further cooling trials. Its removal helped somewhat, even though the craft dropped a small amount in top speed due to worse streamlining. (Grumman)

The XF4F-3 in flight shows powder smudges around the 30-caliber gun barrels just behind the engine cowling. Gun performance was as much a factor in testing as any other aspect of the new aircraft's performance envelope. (Collect Air)

cember 1939. That resulted in further modifications that brought the design to the production configuration commonly thought of as the Wildcat. These changes were most noticeable in the redesign of the vertical fin, which was now rounded off a bit at the tip and blended with a small dorsal fairing into the turtle deck, and the raising of the horizontal tail by about twenty inches from the fuselage centerline onto the fin structure. The rudder horn balance was also enlarged.

Finally, the old BuAer 0383 was delivered to the Navy for the last time on April 23, 1940, looking like a totally different aircraft than when it was first delivered that day in December 1937. The birth of the Wildcat had not been an easy one. On November 7, 1940, the plane was assigned to duty aboard the carrier *Ranger* for familiarization flights by VF-4 pilots. VF-71 and VF-72 pilots on the *Wasp* got a crack at it on December 11 and 12. It was then sent back to the NAS Norfolk where on December 17, 1940, it crashed, killing Lt. (JG) W. C. Johnson, who had apparently turned off the fuel selector valve by mistake instead of actuating the flap selector. The old airframe had 345 hours on it.

By August 8, 1939, however, the Navy had been satisfied with the new fighter and ordered fifty-four F4F-3's. The F4F-3 initially flew in February 1940. However, a few things had turned up that needed to be fixed. The landing gear and tail wheel had to be beefed up, canopy vibration had to be deadened and a bit of longitudinal stability had to be ironed out, as did an excess of carbon monoxide leakage into the cockpit area. The cause of the crash of the prototype was not to be ignored, so the flap handle and fuel valves were moved farther apart. Engine cooling wasn't all it could be, either, and the guns didn't get ammunition fed to them

A closeup of another tack taken by designers to solve the cooling problem while still retaining the large spinner. In this case it was "cuffs," or shaped pieces of sheet metal riveted around the propeller blade shanks, that formed fan blades to cool the engine cylinders. (Grumman)

The XF4F-3 in its near-final configuration, with the large spinner once more a part of the design. Also note that the elevator has been raised several inches onto the vertical fin rather than being mounted on the aft fuselage sides as had been the original configuration. (Grumman)

smoothly when the aircraft was pulling high g combat-type maneuvers. Even some armor plating needed to be added for pilot protection. And one last item: The new production aircraft's top speed did not quite come up to the manufacturer's guarantee; but there wasn't much that could be done about that.

By plane number two, which followed in July, many of the above problems had pretty much been resolved—except for the engine cooling. That was soon addressed by the experts at Langley Field, using the second aircraft as their subject for experimentation. They eventually worked out the answers and those solutions were used on subsequent production aircraft. One hundred eighty-five of the F4F-3 aircraft were built, the last during 1941—before Pearl Harbor. Grumman had also built the first five folding-wing F4F-4's by that time, although they were not yet in Navy service.

The first F4F-3's to see actual service were those delivered to VF-41 December 4, 1940. With yellow wings, red-centered white stars on a blue circle and a gray fuselage, the new planes were a continuation of the gaudy, but nice, coloration of the earlier F3F biplanes.

The next model, numerically, of the Wildcat was the F4F-3A, which was really a redesignation of the F4F-6. It was different than the F4F-3 in that it was fitted with a Pratt & Whitney R-1830-90 Twin Wasp

Views of XF4F-3 in final form at start of F4F-3 production. (Grumman)

fitted with a single-stage two-speed supercharger. This model was later known as Martlet III when taken over by the British Navy. The F4F-4 was, of course, the folding-wing version of the F4F-3. There was also a designation of F4F-4A with an R-1830-90 engine but it was never built. The F4F-4B was another story, as 220 examples were built for a Lend-Lease program and renamed Martlet IV. It had the combination of a Hamilton Standard Hydromatic propeller and a Wright Cyclone engine. Particulars of these and other variants of the Wildcat may be found in chapter ten.

By the time of Pearl Harbor, several Navy and Marine squadrons were equipped with the new Grumman fighters. The Marine units included VMF-121 and -211 (with F4F-3's) and VMF-111 (with F4F-3A's). The VMF-211 machines didn't last long, for the Wildcats' ultimate combat adversary, the Zeros, shot up nine of eleven of the VMF-211 Wildcats during their Pearl Harbor Sunday visit. The Cats at Wake Island were also badly mauled.

Beginning in February 1942 the carriers of the U.S. fleet were on the move, ready to begin the long trip back to regain lost Pacific territory. The Marshall and Gilbert Islands were the first targets of the task force. It used the *Enterprise* and *Yorktown* carriers as a nucleus. The carriers had to be used because the powerful battleships of the Pacific Fleet were either badly damaged or lay on the bottom at Pearl Harbor. With April came the battle of the Coral Sea, a most interesting naval engagement because it was

Side view of F4F-3A. This aircraft was built as a stopgap production fighter while the supercharger used on the F4F-3 had its problems worked out. As a result its performance was not quite as good as that of the F4F-3. (Grumman)

The XF4F-6 was one of a kind, built for the Navy to evaluate the Pratt & Whitney R-1800-90 Twin Wasp engine. (Grumman)

the first time enemy task forces had been engaged without the opposing vessels seeing one another.

Air power had now made itself known in naval engagements. Until then some in high places in the Navy still thought the best naval armada to be comprised of the traditional battleship, cruiser and destroyer formations of earlier years. That type of thinking was proved wrong, once and for all, with the monumental Battle of Midway, which began in early June. It is considered by historians to be the definitive turning point for the Allies in the Pacific in World War II.

It was during this engagement that the folding-wing F4F-4's made their combat debut in strength. The fighters were flown by VF-3 from the *Yorktown,* VF-6 from the *Enterprise,* and VF-8 from the *Hornet.* The latter was now back in regular action after delivering Doolittle's Toyko raiders.

One of the many variants of the Wildcat holds a good deal of interest due mainly to its oddity. That was the F4F-3 pontoon-equipped Wildcatfish. While it is hard to imagine why anyone would want ponderous, drag-inducing pontoons on an agile little fighter plane, there seemed to be reason enough at the time. The Japanese had put a single float under the sleek fuselage of the Zero and a small tip float under each wing. The idea was to have a forward-position fighter available during military beachheads on islands where no airfields were to be found. As such, the floating Zeros were seen in quantity in the Aleutian campaign as well as in the battle for Guadalcanal. They did a fair amount of damage and were around long enough to obtain their own code name, Rufe, instead of the usual Zeke.

The XF4F-8 was a Grumman-built prototype of the General Motors FM-1 Wildcat. (Grumman)

An F4F-4 from VF-41 Ranger. It is marked with oversized stars so that there would be no mistaking it for the red Japanese insignia during May 1942 engagements with the enemy. (U.S. Navy)

Not to be one-upped by the enemy, Edo Corporation was given a contract in autumn of 1942 to convert an F4F-3 into a twin-float seaplane for use in trial operations. In less than three months the craft was delivered for flight tests. Aside from the floats the only other apparent change from the standard was the addition of small supplemental fins to either tip of the stabilizer to help counteract the large "wetted" area at the front of the aircraft due to the rather large proportions of the pontoons. It was not a bad-looking installation, with the heavy streamlined struts joining the two floats to the wings several feet outboard of the fuselage.

Flight testing began February 28, 1943. As with most float-equipped planes, the fuselage sat at a fairly steep angle of attack with relation to the float centerline to allow for the quickest possible liftoff. The nose-high attitude also helped keep the propeller blades out of the water. Testing showed what might be expected. Top speed went down to 266 miles per hour and climb to altitude was on the slow side. It didn't really matter, though, for only one was built.

The business end of an F4F-4 as seen by the enemy during a head-on attack by the Grumman fighter. (U.S. Navy)

However, in their heat-of-the-moment impetuousness, the Navy's public relations folks had the Wildcatfish raising general hell with the Japanese Zero in the far South Pacific. What was *really* happening was that the Seabees were going in with tremendous amounts of heavy equipment and carving usable airstrips out of the jungles in such short periods that there was no need for the inferior-performance float-fighter to even make the scene. The trial model was soon returned to wheel configuration so that it *could* be made use of in the war. However, the floatplane has been an interesting diversion from the general production lineage of the Wildcat.

Other areas of Grumman's experimentation during the Wildcat production period included the fighter being towed behind B-17's and A-20's as a means of stretching their range. Another experiment that didn't work very well was the fitting of one ship with electric flaps instead of the vacuum-operated ones used on the regular-production machines. During tests only one flap lowered—the other one stayed up. Results? Instant roll on approach, instant prang, instant end of program!

Another idea that worked out better was the frangible wingtip scheme. The thought here was that under high g loadings only the outer three and a half feet of the wings would break off—the dewinging would not occur at the roots, as was more customary and disastrous. This new method still allowed enough flying surface to maybe limp home. Also the wing could be built several hundred pounds lighter—increasing the aircraft's performance. While never adopted on the Wildcat or Hellcat production aircraft, the idea was incorporated in the much later F8F Bearcats, the last of the Grumman piston-engine fighters.

There is a photograph, seen on occasion, of a Wildcat fitted with super-long wings, sort of like a bulbous prop-driven U-2. While no source seems to have any recollection of what it was for, it seems almost certain its use was to be the same as the U-2: super-long-range high altitude recon work.

Grumman had Wildcat production rolling so well that by the end of 1942, 1,169 of the folding-wing F4F-4's had been delivered to the Navy and the Marines. Along with the folding wings, for carrier storage, there

A peaceful shot of the F4F-3A in flight. (National Archives)

were some other niceties in store for the pilot of the -4 model. A very important one was the addition of a good amount of armor. The bullet-resistant windshield alone was made of twenty-five pounds of high-strength glass. Installed behind the pilot's seat were ninety-four pounds of armor, with another forty-five pounds in front of the engine oil tank. Beneath the cockpit floor was the self-sealing fuel tank which, believe it or not, offered substantial protection from bullets coming from that direction. Only from the sides and directly above was the pilot unprotected. There he relied on his vision to keep him out of trouble. All in all, the pilot was encased in a pretty rugged little battle trench and this certainly helped him gain confidence in a combat situation. The six fifty-caliber Browning M-1's in the wings, with 240 rounds per gun, likewise gave him confidence to dish it out under combat situations.

Since, with the tremendous production of Wildcats from Grumman, all Navy shipboard fighter squadrons were soon equipped with the Wildcat, one would have thought all was well with the Navy, fighterwise. Not so. The A6M2 Japanese Zero bettered the F4F-4 in almost every aspect of range, climb and maneuverability, to say nothing of the valuable factor of a superior top speed. The Zero's service ceiling was higher, its turning radius smaller, its diving speed about equal and its stalling speed lower. It can make one wonder why the Wildcat was still a great fighter and not a total flop in combat.

There were two reasons. The first was that it obviously was the only Navy fighter the U.S. had in those bleak days. Therefore *any* success it had was bound to be looked on with a certain degree of national pride. Reason number two was that tactics were soon developed by the Navy and Marine pilots that could sort of equalize things. However, this was more as a result of the pilots' skills and training coupled with outstanding shows of courage.

A Grumman J2F-6 Duck stands by while its Wildcat brother blows smoke in its face during a JATO carrier takeoff. Commander L. G. Simpler was at the controls and the date was March 18, 1944. Note hard right rudder to correct engine torque. Aircraft was the same as used by Captain Gore. (U.S. Navy)

Captain W. Gore makes a jet-assisted takeoff (JATO) test in a Wildcat. Rocket bottle is fastened under the fuselage. (National Air & Space Museum)

As in any combat the idea is to take advantage of weaknesses shown by an opponent and at the same time make the most of one's own strong points. That's what Wildcat pilots did. They attempted to gain an initial altitude advantage, dive through the enemy formations shooting up anything they could, then make a rapid pullup to zoom once more for height above the enemy. Fortunately, the Zeros flamed easily due to their lack of armor plate and self-sealing tanks. Those weight-saving shortcomings were a large part of the reason for their hot performance. The Navy and Marines got away with their new tactics in the Pacific, whereas against the Me-109's in Europe such tactics would have been suicide.

The General Motors FM-2 was built in the largest numbers of all Wildcats and is easily recognized by the larger than normal fin and rudder. This was done to counteract the increased torque of the Wright Cyclone engine during low air speed waveoffs from the small "Jeep" carriers from which the FM-2 normally flew. (National Air & Space Museum)

The F4F's squared-off appearance, if one didn't look too closely, sometimes got enemy fighter pilots in deep trouble. The larger Grumman TBF Avenger had a shape somewhat similar to that of the Wildcat from a distance. Hapless Japanese pilots sometimes made high-speed dives at what appeared to be formations of unwary Wildcats cruising below. Upon appraching their tails, running in at high speeds for the kill, the Japanese would suddenly notice something strange about their victims-to-be. Mounted atop the Avengers' fuselages were gun turrets, each sporting twin fifties! Too late—the collective, heavy-caliber machine guns were trained directly on them. The Zeros disintegrated around the attacker in a hail of lead. It didn't take long before the enemy looked more carefully to see if his target was a Wildcat or an Avenger.

The Wildcat continued to stave off the Japanese until 1943 when the Grumman Hellcat F6F-3's began to appear in large quantities. Those new Grumman fighters were designed from the outset to make mincemeat of the Zeros. That was a mission they promptly began to perform once they entered combat.

Grumman stopped making F4F's with the start of Hellcat production, and Wildcats quickly became the domain of the General Motors Corporation. At Grumman there had been little overlap between the Wildcat and Hellcat. Grumman production of the F4F stopped in May 1943 after 1,971 of them.

Once the Wildcats were out of front-line carrier operations they were still not out of the war. Wildcats, both the early Grumman machines and the General Motors versions (FM-1 and FM-2), were put to work on the light escort carriers. The Jeep Carriers, as they were called, were used to keep an eye on and destroy enemy submarines in both the Atlantic and Pacific theaters. Antisubmarine protection was truly needed; for the supply lines to both Europe and the South Pacific were thousands of miles long and the military appetite for equipment during the battles waged on

Cartridge start of a new FM-2 at the Linden, New Jersey, General Motors plant. Photograph was taken from the control tower. (National Air & Space Museum)

both fronts was horrendous. This meant that Henry Kaiser's Victory Ships, and anything else that floated, were pressed into use to carry the supplies of arms, soldiers and other equipment needed to wage a now offensive war.

Curtiss-Wright helped out somewhat with the Wildcats' new mission with the convoy escort carriers. Since the escort carriers' flight decks were much shorter than a normal carrier, it was important to make the aircraft lighter so they were better able to take off and land in short distances with more room for error. Curtiss-Wright came up with the R-1820-56 Cyclone, a single-row, nine-cylinder radial with a two-speed supercharger. With new-technology forged cylinder heads, the new Cyclone weighed in some 230 pounds lighter than the Pratt & Whitney Twin Wasps that were powering the F4F-4's and at the same time belted out 1,350 horsepower—150 more than the Pratt & Whitney. The engine change resulted in the Grumman XF4F-8 that carried only four fifties instead of the usual six, a further weight savings. With the increased engine torque the new Wildcat model got a taller vertical fin and rudder with an increase in area to help out in the event of a sudden waveoff during landing.

All these new features were put in the FM-2 design, the General Motors Eastern Aircraft Division's version of the XF4F-8 Wildcat. General Motors, as a result of the new model, came up with the long end of the stick as far as Wildcat production went (profit money, too!). The bottom line, at the end of the war, showed that GM had completed 5,927 of the chubby little fighters out of the 7,898 that were built—seventy-five percent of them! Not bad for a company that had only built automobiles a few

This F4F-4 being launched from the fight deck of the USS *Charger* shows the Wildcat as it should be, full of life, full of flight. (National Archives)

years before. From its auto years General Motors had become expert at the business of high production of complicated machines on an assembly line and here it really showed. The escort carrier jobs remained until war's end and the company continued to build Wildcats for that use until August 1945.

The earlier F4F's and subsequent FM's had their victories, particularly against Japanese transport aircraft and bombers in the early days of the war. They were still kept useful, but more on the back burner of the action during the latter days of the war. Those were the days of the escort fighters protecting the airspace over the many convoys needed to supply the front lines.

Once the war was over, however, the F4F's and FM's rapidly disappeared from the scene. There were several reasons for this: The first was the then prevalent Hellcat, which was a far superior aircraft to the Wildcat. Second, the new jet age was soon to wipe out the usefulness of even the Hellcat. Finally, there was just no use for either. They were remnants of a type of war never to be fought again. Today a few remain in museums around the world, and, if you really luck out, you might see a restored one at a gathering of warbirds, such as at Oshkosh, Wisconsin.

To backtrack a little, while the Wildcats were holding off the Japanese in the early stages of the Pacific war they were likewise helping out in the Allied European efforts. The first British Fleet Air Arm Squadron to be equipped with the fighter was number 892 on July 15, 1942. The F4F's, (Martlets) were placed aboard the escort carriers *Archer* and *Battler*. During the invasion of North Africa the Martlet IV's of numbers 881 and 882 Squadrons off the carriers *Illustrious* and *Victorious* took part. One of the Martlets of 882 accepted the surrender of the French airfield at Blida. The pilot, while on patrol over the enemy fighter field, noticed that the French below were making motions that he should land. He did, and

A loose formation flight of Wildcats on a quiet late afternoon mission, the airman's world at its best. (National Air & Space Museum)

F4F-4 taking off from the USS *Wolverine* (IX-64) at sunset in March 1943. Note the lowered flaps and hard right rudder used during the maneuver. (U.S. Navy)

there was the field's commandant waiting to present him with a formal surrender!

During the seesaw struggle with Rommel's Africa Korps, the Wildcat fighter (designed to operate in a nautical environment) operated in North Africa's Sahara Desert with number 805 Squadron located at Dekheil.

One of the early Wildcat units that went to sea with the Royal Navy was 802 Squadron aboard the escort carrier HMS *Audacity* in Sep-

The F4F-3S Wildcatfish taxies for maiden flight, takes off and is airborne. To make up for the large float side area forward, extra fins were added to the stabilizer tips. By the time the aircraft had arrived at Norfolk NAS in June 1943, a large ventral fin was also added. (National Archives)

tember 1941. The big carrier was being used to escort a Gibraltar-bound convoy. Just as flies are attracted to honey, submarines are attracted to big convoys. On September 19 the Martlets discovered a lurking German sub. The Martlets let go with their fifties and the sub was forced to dive to avoid being sunk.

The next day was a good one too. The Martlets blew a Focke-Wulfe FW-200 four-engine recon plane from the skies near the convoy as it shadowed the ships' movements and reported their position to the U-boat commanders in the area. That was pretty good work for the Martlets, but on the *Audacity*'s second voyage the Grummans really got down to

The one-of-a-kind F4F-3S Wildcatfish was to be the Navy's answer to the Japanese Zero floatplanes (code named Rufe). The rapidity with which the Seabees built new airfields on Pacific islands made its use unnecessary. (Collect Air)

business and destroyed four Focke-Wulfe FW-200's during a thirty-hour period. Afterward a few of them had to land in the dark. That was tough enough, but on a deck that was rolling fourteen degrees?

All in all the British were quite taken with the Martlet during their war efforts in Africa and the Middle East. The later models even saw service with British units operating in the Far East, the Pacific and East Indies.

While the aircraft was designed for carrier duties it also served well as a front-line, land-based fighter as will be seen in the next chapter, which deals with the legendary career of Joe Foss, Marine ace. In the South Pacific, island warfare was conducted from airfields hacked out of the jungles by Seabees. Carrier aircraft were launched to occupy those forward outposts in support of ground troop operations.

The Wildcat came through. When the end-of-war bean counting was complete, it was found to be a pretty good all-around performer. The U.S. Navy credited the type with 905 enemy aircraft destroyed during combat operations versus a loss of 178 Wildcats from 1941 to 1943, or about five to one. For the entire war, the ratio was about seven to one.

CHAPTER IV

FOSS AND OTHER WILDCAT WARRIORS

The Congressional Medal of Honor, the highest award for bravery that can be bestowed on an American, is not easy to come by. Navy and Marine Wildcat pilots garnered eight of those coveted medals. A brief review of each of their tales of exceptional heroism is certainly worth relating.

On December 8, 1941, at Wake Island, seven of VMF-211's twelve Wildcats were destroyed on the ground by the Japanese preparing for the invasion of that outpost. An eighth fighter escaped the wrath of the thirty-six twin-engine Japanese Bettys that took the airstrip by surprise from behind a squall line. Even that aircraft's auxiliary fuel tank was wrecked. The other four of the twelve Marine fighters were on combat air patrol searching for an enemy attack that was sure to come. They had been alerted shortly before by the decoded message, "Hickham Field has been attacked by Jap dive bombers! This is the real thing." Unfortunately, the Bettys had managed to slip under and past them for their attack.

One of the four remaining airborne Wildcats crashed during its landing on the Wake airstrip after the attack—due to the bomb craters left by the Bettys. That left only four serviceable aircraft out of the twelve that had flown off the USS *Enterprise* on December 4 to bolster the island stronghold that marked the farthest U.S. outpost in the Pacific. Along with the aircraft, the Marine fighter squadron also had lost sixty percent of its men on the ground and two large stores of aviation fuel during the attack.

The four remaining aircraft continued to fight for several days and they even managed to rout the first Japanese invasion attempt on December 11, working closely with the Marines' shore-gun batteries. On December 11 the Japanese decided they could storm the island's rocky beaches after being assured that the American air defenses were demolished. Twenty American 100-pound aerial bombs and 20,000 American fifty-caliber rounds later, the Japanese realized that there was still a bit of air power to be reckoned with on Wake.

While many of the American bombs had struck and damaged the invasion support ships, there was one instance of even greater interest and consequence: A bomb dropped by USMC Capt. Henry T. Elrod fell on a store of depth charges on the deck of the Japanese destroyer *Kisaragi*.

Two F4F-3's from VF-3 aboard the USS *Saratoga*. In the foreground is LCDR John S. Thach and in the background is Lt. Edward H. "Butch" O'Hare. The squadron's Felix The Cat insignia is on both aircraft and Thach's plane carries three rising-sun victory markings. Note also the difference in rudder markings. (U.S. Navy)

The whole ship exploded and the enemy was down one destroyer. The price of battle had to be paid though. Elrod's Wildcat was badly damaged in the wild encounter and was totaled during his ensuing landing back at Wake. Meanwhile, a second Wildcat was wrecked in a takeoff accident during the heat of battle. Now there were but two Wildcats left.

However, the Wake defenders were cheered by the damage they had inflicted on the invasion attempt. Between the fighters and the shore batteries, they had sunk two destroyers, wrecked portions of eight other ships and killed about 700 of the enemy personnel. Later the same day, a surfaced enemy submarine was sunk by a Wildcat. The Grumman fighters were on a roll, for a short while at least.

The Japanese, with relentless aerial attacks and a much larger carrier-reinforced invasion fleet, continued the attack. Those last two Wildcats soon went down. Only, however, after they had been fixed and refixed, by ground crews utilizing spare parts from the crashed or destroyed F4F's strewn about the airstrip. Those two Wildcats even managed to shoot down a few more enemy aircraft during their last days in the air.

The USS *Wasp,* CVA-7, was host to this amazing collection of F4F-3's, F4F-4's and roundel carrying Spitfires with desert air filters fitted. It was all in preparation for the North African campaign in April 1942. (U.S. Navy)

After fifteen days of aerial resistance, VMF-211 was fresh out of aircraft. The remaining pilots and ground crews then turned themselves over to the infantry forces of the Marines to continue in the fight to defend the island. On December 23, Captain Elrod was among the survivors who fought the new invasion in hand-to-hand combat. He bravely manned a machine gun and sent many enemy troops to their deaths before he too was killed. For his hard fighting, both in the air and on the island battleground, he was awarded the Congressional Medal of Honor posthumously.

With the war continuing in earnest in 1942 the United States tried to not only stem the Japanese invasion tide but reverse it as well. The next Medal of Honor bestowed on a Wildcat pilot went to USMC Lt. Col. Harold W. Bauer of VMF-212, for his efforts on Guadalcanal September 28, October 3 and October 16, 1942. Flying an F3F-3 he destroyed four Japanese planes; then on the sixteenth he bagged four more Val bombers, even though he was almost out of fuel. All in all, he did in eleven enemy aircraft before he was killed in action November 11, 1942. That was Armistice Day, commemorating the end of the war to end all wars in 1918. . . .

F4F-4 at Henderson Field, Guadalcanal. Those rising-sun victory markings on the fuselage sides add up to 19 victories. Perhaps the plane was flown by Joe Foss who racked up 26 victories. (National Archives)

Another recipient of the coveted medal was USMC 1st Lt. Jefferson J. DeBlanc of VMF-112. He eventually wound up the war with nine victories, almost enough to make him a double ace. Flying a Wildcat he led a four-plane formation during a Solomon Island encounter with the enemy on January 31, 1942. He succeeded in downing three floatplanes and two Zeros before having to bail out of his own shot-up and falling aircraft. By putting up this fight he made it possible for U.S. Navy dive and torpedo bombers to press home their attacks totally unmolested by the enemy.

USMC Maj. Robert Galer, of VMF-224, ended the war with thirteen confirmed victories and received the medal for aggressive combat in August and September 1942 during the Guadalcanal invasion by the United States. It was a time when aggressive leaders were badly needed to show the way to victory as the Allies went on the offensive against the Japanese. Such leadership was quickly rewarded by a grateful nation.

One of the best known of the Medal of Honor winners was USN Lt. Edward (Butch) O'Hare after whom the giant Chicago airport is named. He was a section leader of an F4F-3 squadron flying CAP (combat air patrol), with a wingman, from the *Lexington,* as it patrolled off Rabaul, on February 20, 1943. He shot down five Japanese Betty bombers, three at the same time! This so terrorized the other attacking bombers they quickly fled the scene. He was later lost while flying a night-fighter mission in a Hellcat.

O'Hare's Medal of Honor came through and was presented posthumously. The official citation read, in part, ". . . having lost the assistance of his team mates, he interposed his plane between his ship and an advancing enemy formation of nine twin-engine heavy bombers. Without hesitation, alone and unaided, he repeatedly attacked the enemy formation at close range in the face of their combined machine gun and cannon fire, and despite their concentrated opposition, he, by his gallant and courageous action, his extremely skillful marksmanship and making the most of his limited amount of ammunition, shot down five enemy bombers and severely damaged a sixth before they reached the bomb release point." His more immediate reward was a promotion to lieutenant commander.

Another Medal of Honor recipient was USMC 1st Lt. James E. Swett, who was an excellent marksman on April 7, 1942. That day he shot

A couple of Douglas SBD Dauntless dive bombers get ready to roll past folded-wing F4F-4's that are being serviced. (National Air & Space Museum)

down eight Val bombers. He ignored flack from the American ships below and shot down three. Then, putting the other attackers to flight, he shot down five more. It all happened in only fifteen minutes! The wear and tear on his aircraft during the fight forced him to ditch his Wildcat at the end of the episode. Later, he also performed very aggressively when it came to downing enemy planes. He ended the war with a total of 16½ planes to his credit.

USMC Maj. John L. Smith, squadron commander of VMF-223, ended the war in the Pacific with a fat nineteen victories. His medal, however, was won early on in the war, between August 21 and September 15, 1942, during a combat tour at Guadalcanal—a tremendously hard-fought battle.

That takes care of seven of the eight Wildcat pilots who were Congressional Medal of Honor winners. Then there was USMC Capt. Joseph J. Foss of VMF-121. His claim to fame was that he really beat the hell out of enemy aircraft in the early days of the war in the Pacific. His career culminated in his knocking off twenty-six of the enemy's aircraft and equaling Capt. Eddie Rickenbacker's World War I record for planes shot down. Rickenbacker, till that time, was America's ace of aces and, of course, a national hero. Foss received the medal from President Frank-

FM-1's (same as F4F-4's except built by General Motors) were built between September 1942 and fall 1943—839 in all. (U.S. Navy)

lin D. Roosevelt in Washington, D.C., in recognition of his efforts in action from October 9, 1942, to January 25, 1943. Here is how his scorecard read.

Hunting the enemy in his Wildcat, Foss polished off four Zeros on October 23, another four on the twenty-fifth and still another three on November 7. That day he got in a bit of a pickle himself, for his Wildcat was shot out of the skies by the always able enemy. There were, of course, some ones and twos in his victory roster mixed in among these major accomplishments. On January 3, 1943, he downed three more enemy aircraft and there he was, the equal as a fighter pilot to the immortal Rickenbacker. His story is worth exploring more.

Foss was in action a total of sixty-three days. During that time he literally ripped the South Pacific skies apart. He was finally a casualty of malaria rather than any enemy bullet. A South Dakota farm boy, he was not unusual in his ability with guns; Foss hunted with great success. His real talent showed up in shooting birds, which later equated itself to the fine art of shooting enemy warbirds. Twenty of his victims were Zeros. They had outclassed the Wildcat all during the war's early days but, in the skilled hands of Foss, the bulky little F4F came on strong and the myth of the invincible Zero didn't hold any longer.

In many respects Foss' life was the typical all-American story of the hard-working Midwest farm boy who made good. His first two years of education were at a country school, before continuing in the town of Sioux Falls, South Dakota. He played alto saxophone in the high school band that, incidentally, was good enough to play at the 1933 Century of Progress Exposition in Chicago. He also spent a lot of time hunting. It was a family-and-friends type of thing everyone just did. Foss became good at it. (A little investigation shows that most of our aces had hunting backgrounds.)

His father died in an accident during Foss' senior year in high school. As a result, in addition to getting an education, he had to run the

Six F4F-4's cruise in a loose echelon formation. (Collect Air)

family farm. That fall he entered Augustana College in Sioux Falls. He lasted one year. Out of money, it was back to full-time farming, but that didn't work out either because of a drought. To make ends meet he then obtained a job at the Morrell meat packing plant in Sioux Falls. After a year, he realized that meat packing was going to be a tough way to make a living. The only way out was to go back to college and complete his education. He enrolled at Sioux Falls College, making a little money by working as a janitor. In 1939 he transferred to the University of South Dakota as a junior, this time working in a meat market, waiting tables and washing dishes in a fraternity house to pay the way. With income from those efforts and selling his car and some farmland he had inherited, he got through. The Depression days of the thirties were tough but then, he was a tough guy.

With the busy schedule, when did aviation become a part of his life? Well, Lindbergh did it again. The great American hero arrived at the Sioux Falls airport in the *Spirit of St. Louis* in 1927, on a tour of the United States following his Atlantic crossing to Paris. That started it. Next, in 1930, a squadron of Marine planes came to town, performing during an air show and teaching the locals what formation flying was all about. That kept it going.

In 1934 Foss took his first plane ride in one of the typical rickety barnstormers that seemed to always be kicking around the Midwest in the thirties. These flying incidents teased him and, finally, in 1937, after scraping together the required $75, he soloed in a Taylorcraft—the predecessor of the well-known J-3 Cub. After that he flew when he could afford the plane rental, a hefty six bucks an hour.

The final development was a Civil Aeronautics Administration course during his senior year at college. That included seventy-two hours of ground school and fifty-eight hours of flying. With a degree in business administration plus his flight training and experience he was a natural candidate for Marine aviation. It was 1940 and the services were starting their buildup in earnest.

In June 1940 Foss was assigned a short twelve-hour course in a light plane in Minneapolis, which supposedly taught him to solo. He didn't bother mentioning to them that he already had several hundred flight hours. It was then off to Pensacola, Florida, for the full military pilot treatment: endless ground school, lots of military discipline, and some flight training. At least that was the way it appeared to most of the student pilots.

By the time he was through flight school Foss was twenty-seven. He was initially assigned as an instructor, then later to a recon squadron

F4F, with hook down, makes a final approach and is drawn to a stop aboard the carrier USS *Ranger*. (National Archives)

aboard a carrier. That was not what he wanted at all, but the noncombatant assignments were probably because of his advanced age. He wanted to be a *fighter* pilot. He finally got his way and was assigned as executive officer to VMF-121 in California, August 1, 1942. He was then promoted to captain, and before the end of August he was on his way to the South Pacific combat zone.

On October 7, 1942, flying Wildcats, Foss and portions of VMF-121 left a small transport carrier's deck and headed over water toward Henderson Field, Guadalcanal. The uneventful flight from the carrier took a few hours, with the only problem occurring when the fighter contingent landed on the bomber flight strip. They were warmly welcomed but were requested to take off and go over to the fighter strip, only a mile's hop away. VMF-121, and Foss, were now officially at war with the Japanese.

Foss' first week on the island was spent lying awake nights, while the enemy shelled the American installations, and flying sorties during the day as Japanese bombers came over in swarms to try to knock out Allied positions. On October 13, Foss and his wingman rose to meet a

Here's a landing accident aboard an escort carrier in 1942 just prior to the North African campaign. It seems to have everyone's attention. (U.S. Navy)

group of bombers. A Zero, hiding in the clouds, surprised Foss. Tracers flew past the F4F's cockpit as the diving enemy sped past. That was when the Zero made its big mistake. It recovered from its dive by pulling up directly in front of Foss' six fifties. Foss gave him a burst and the attacker became an instant fireball. That was number one. Foss was scared, excited and ready for another when a new batch of Zeros really got on him and chased him back to his field.

After a night of lying in a foxhole during constant naval bombardment, Foss was again in a position to clobber a Zero. This time the enemy fighter was hot after another Wildcat and never even noticed it was flying across Foss' gunsight. It was *not* a case of live-and-learn for the Japanese pilot! Several more days went by, during which the main action was strafing supply barges and any other target of opportunity the Grumman fighters happened upon.

On October 18, Foss again became entangled with enemy Zeros. This time he really got in the swing of things, blowing one up as it began to attack one of his buddies, and then a second one during a hair-raising head-on game of chicken. By that time the mainstream of Japanese bombers, protected by the Zeros, had arrived on the scene. Foss made a couple of quick passes through their formation and finally managed to bag one from below. He hit the bomber's fuel tanks and the enemy plane blew up instantly. That made five down and glory. Foss was now an ace. It wasn't all that much fun, though, as Foss' Wildcat was out of ammunition, low on gas and being chased by a swarm of Zeros when he landed.

F4F-4's at Guadalcanal's Henderson Field, 1942. (Collect Air)

After all that activity, the next day the fighter group took a day off to wash clothes and chew the rag with some of the ground troops. However, the following day Foss and company were in the air again to try to head off an approaching flight of eighteen Zeros. It was a head-on attack and one of the enemy started firing at Foss as he closed the distance. When a collision was imminent the Zero broke away to one side. That was all Foss needed. He banked the F4F hard over and onto the opponent's tail. Seconds later it was all over for the hapless Zero. Almost immediately another Zero locked horns with Foss. After several passes at each other Foss got him with an old bird-hunter's deflection shot. The twentieth of October went down as a good day for Foss—he now had seven planes to his credit—but it was not as good as the twenty-third would be.

Foss and company scrambled at noon to intercept a flight of sixteen enemy bombers intent on pounding the Allied ships in the harbor. The bombers were, of course, escorted by the ever-protective Zeros. It was only a few minutes before the skies were alive with dogfights as Zeros and Wildcats began to tangle. Foss bagged four of the enemy but he took a batch of hits himself in the process and, to make matters worse, he was fresh out of ammunition! He had been in combat less than two weeks and had eleven enemy planes notched on his guns. And it went on like that.

On the twenty-fifth Foss dropped *five* fireballed Zeros from the blue South Pacific skies. It was a long hard day of dogfighting for Foss, but that day was also almost the end. When he returned to base there were bullet holes in his headrest. He couldn't have gotten much closer to being killed than that.

Lest it be thought this whole thing was easy for the Americans it must be realized that while Joe Foss and other aces like him were raising hell with the enemy, the enemy was getting its licks in too with the downing of many American pilots during the high-geared battles. There were some Japanese aces who blew plenty of Wildcats out of the air, particularly if the Wildcat pilot was new and green to the job; or, as in a few cases, was not meant to be a fighter pilot. The Japanese had nerve and it was backed up by the high-stepping Zero. The nimble little fighter couldn't take it as well as the Wildcat when it came to getting shot at, but it could sure dish it out.

At that time the Japanese pilots had months of combat experience, dating all the way back to the China campaign in some cases. They looked down their noses at the Americans—almost as much as the Americans felt they were superior to the Japanese. Such is war and the effect of propaganda on the troops. Neither of the combatants had the full story of their enemy's weaknesses or strengths.

JV-579 was an FM-1, of which General Motors built 312. Shown here in invasion stripes, the craft flew close support missions for the Allies during that historic event. (National Air & Space Museum)

After October 25, both sides were weary and the air activity relaxed a bit. Some days Foss and friends rose to meet an enemy attack but the enemy fled. Other days they didn't even make contact because the weather was so bad. That also resulted in some hair-raising near-zero/zero landings (zero visibility—horizontally and vertically) for the pilots. Even without the presence of the enemy there was still danger.

November 7 was another big day for Foss—he went down at sea; surely a memorable event in any fighter pilot's career. By this time he had sixteen enemy planes to his credit and, though careful, was probably starting to feel more than confident of his prowess in battle. The group was ordered to attack a small Japanese naval attack force consisting of some destroyers and a light cruiser. On the way to the attack the Wildcats made contact with a flight of Zeros and within a minute or so Foss had an addition to his record. After that, his flight made contact with a couple of biplane recon-types scouting with the enemy. He got them both but not before one of the scout's rear cockpit gunners got off some shots of his own, opening up the Wildcat's cockpit to the high-speed airstream. By this time everyone else had headed home and Foss found himself alone and a little lost, with an ugly tropical storm looming in the direction of where he reckoned his base on Guadalcanal to be.

After trying to avoid the squall he found that his engine suddenly refused to cooperate. First it smoked, then it quit. Gliding toward the nearest island he rode the F4F down to an airframe-wrecking ditch a few miles offshore. He was thrown underwater, his chute hampering his efforts to get to the surface. Finally, after hours in the water he was rescued by some friendly missionaries on the island. After a few days he was picked up by a PBY and returned to his group on Guadalcanal. The adventure had added seventeen, eighteen and nineteen to his row of victories.

After a few days of quiet, Foss rose again to battle a group of torpedo bombers about to attack a large American task force in the area. In a short time he had sent one of the intruders down in flames. As he was about to get a bead on another of the bombers, a Zero attacked him. But it made the mistake of overrunning its quarry. Foss quickly turned him into an exploding fireball then continued pressing his attack on the bomber. He got it too. With that he skirted the fight, avoiding any more attacking Zeros. He was out of ammunition and a dogfight was no place for a fighter

A classic shot of the FM-2 built by General Motors. (National Air & Space Museum)

pilot with that malady. Three more planes had been shot down and his score was now twenty-two.

Two days later, on November 17, Foss bagged an easy one—another Japanese recon plane. It didn't die so easily, though. The rear gunner was still blazing away at Foss when the plane hit the drink. While the Japanese couldn't seem to down him, malaria could; and it hit full force the next day. That was the end of combat for the veteran fighter pilot for a while. It was off to R and R on New Caledonia.

By January 15, 1943, he was back in the air again with a pent-up urge to start adding to his score again. He did. Three more Zeros! That did it. He had now tied the immortal Rickenbacker and the brass in Washington said that was enough. They had an honest-to-goodness war hero on their hands and they didn't want to risk his getting shot down by some stray dogfight bullet. He flew for a while longer while Washington ironed out the red tape, then started the long trip home. The strange thing was that he was unaware of Rickenbacker's score and what a super-hero he was until he arrived in D.C. After that, it was the full treatment culminating in the presentation of the Congressional Medal of Honor by President Franklin Roosevelt.

These men were top U.S. Marine and Navy fighter pilots as far as the Congressional Medal of Honor goes but there were many more aces who received less recognition but still could thank the Wildcat for carrying them in and out of battle with victory and honor at a time when the Navy and Marines really had nothing else to offer in the way of a fighter plane to stop the Japanese in the Pacific.

Another early Wildcat pilot of note, for example, was Lt. Commander John S. Thach, leader of VF-3. He was the one who came up with the famous Thach Weave technique of mutual protection. This tactic, borrowed from scout-bomber pilots, was where two Wildcats flew close together and criss-crossed each other's tail for the duration of a combat patrol. Prior to this, Navy pilots were airborne in six-plane flights with two sub-groups of three each—sitting ducks for a swarm of Zeros. The new formation was used during the rest of the war, commencing about the time the F4F-4 folding-wing variant made its debut in numbers at Midway.

The Wildcat was a tough bird when used right—get in, shoot fast and get out. Under those conditions the aircraft could, and did, raise havoc with the best-laid enemy plans. They could do most any combat chore except win in a dogfight with Zeros!

ZERO HOUR— JAPANESE STYLE

CHAPTER V

It was only a short while after Pearl Harbor that the American public began to hear about a fantastic super fighter the supposed backward Japanese seemed to have. Most laymen were surprised and appalled that such a thing could have happened. They had seen pictures of the Japanese Air Force battling the Chinese in *Life* magazine and in the Paramount movie newsreels that were the "eyes and ears of the world." From *those* sources there wasn't anything that looked very mysterious about Japanese fighter aircraft. They all seemed rather archaic, in fact, with their large elliptical wings, huge spatted fixed landing gears, long greenhouse pilot enclosures and all-white paint jobs. Those awkward-looking aircraft would certainly be no match for our slick P-40's and the new Bell P-39 Airacobras, then coming on line and seen in the same newsreels. Zero—it sure sounded mysterious.

The big surprise was the result of the Japanese pulling off just about the most successful snow-job the world has ever seen. When Westerners, newsmen and military people had been allowed to see examples of the Japanese Air Force, the Japanese had always been careful to show them only their older planes. That carefully nurtured the West's belief that the Japanese were way behind in designing and building military aircraft.

When the Zero showed up in combat—in quantity—we began to learn what a hot fighter really was. In the war's initial dogfights the poor guys in Wildcats never knew what hit them.

The U.S. didn't know about the Zero, even though it had made its combat debut over Chungking China on September 13, 1940. Zipping down from 27,000 feet the Zeros swept twenty-seven defending Chinese fighters from the skies within minutes. In the months that followed they did likewise—every time Chinese aircraft were encountered—and not one Zero was lost.

General Claire Chenault, leader of the A.V.G., or Flying Tigers, attempted to convey to his superiors in the U.S. that such an aircraft existed. However, the Japanese smoke screen over the Zero had been so successful that the U.S. brass chose not to listen to Chenault. The first the U.S. saw of a Zero was when they came pouring out of the blue Hawaiian sky that Sunday morning, December 7.

The early concept for the new aircraft was outlined by the Japanese Navy in a requirement letter dated October 5, 1937. When reviewed by fighter designers of the Nippon aircraft industry they must have thought their Navy brass had been influenced by too much Sake when they drafted it. The Navy wanted a maximum speed exceeding 310 miles per hour, fast for a 1937 fighter—even a land-based one—and everybody

The Zero was the nemesis of the Wildcat during the early days of World War II. It was faster as well as more nimble, and therefore certainly not to be engaged in a dogfight. (National Archives)

knew *they* were faster than the carrier-based variety! The requirements specified the range and maneuverability to exceed any existing fighter. In 3.5 minutes the new machine had to be pushing 10,000 feet. With all that performance the Navy wanted the plane to be a potent gun-slinger also. It asked for an armament of two cannon and two machine guns.

There was no question it was a tall order and when it arrived for study at the Nakajima and Mitsubishi engineering departments it didn't take Nakajima engineers long to decide it was too much for them to handle. At a design meeting on January 17, 1938, they officially withdrew. Not so with the Mitsubishi people, however. Mr. Jiro Horikoshi was chief designer of Mitsubishi Jukogyo K.K. He had decided that the only way to attempt the job was to throw caution to the winds and create the new fighter by pushing every conceiveable portion of the design to the cutting edge of aerial technology.

The first step was to select an engine; after much reasoning, the Zuisei Type 13 was chosen. (The name for the engine translates to "auspicious star.") It was a fourteen-cylinder twin-row radial that could put out 750 horsepower, sort of anemic by the standards of the Wrights and Pratt & Whitneys of the time. However, Horikoshi felt the power would be sufficient if the airframe was designed light enough—and low weight would certainly help the maneuverability too. The engine was very light and of a small diameter, which made it possible to reduce frontal area, one of the most important considerations when streamlining an airframe.

A two-blade constant-speed propeller was the next selection. It was a new device. It allowed the engine to develop maximum power at all times, regardless of the aircraft's speed. Extreme care was taken in the design of the airframe. Weight control was even more important than speed for maneuverability, when the relatively low-horsepower engine was considered. The design was so fussy that adding anything weighing

The Mitsubishi A6M2 Zero held an almost mysterious aura for the Allies until one fell into their hands. Flight evaluation soon showed it to be quite lightly built, though very fast and agile. (National Archives)

more than 1/100,000 of the aircraft's final weight was carefully considered.

One new item that helped a great deal was the development of a new aluminum alloy known as ESD (Extra-Super Duralum). This new light and tough alloy was developed by Sumitomo Metal Industry Company. Upon investigation, it was established that with this alloy over thirty kilograms of weight could be saved in the wing spar alone! Before it could be used, however, special permission had to be acquired from the Japanese Navy. It was granted and, eventually, over 3,000 drawings later, the fighter design was complete for building a prototype.

It was a nifty-looking fighter! Starting with a small spinner covering the constant-speed propeller hub, the fuselage began with a close-fitting cowl over the radial engine. That was the largest diameter of the fuselage and it faired nearly straight back with only minimal outward curves to the pointed tail cone. A few feet back from the engine was the pilot's enclosure, shaped like a modern bubble canopy. While plastics technology of the time did not allow a true bubble canopy to be blown, (à la P-51D), this similar shape had its advantages: 360° cockpit visibility and great streamlining. Overall length of the fuselage was only twenty-nine feet nine inches.

The thirty-two-foot one-inch span wings provided nearly 230 square feet of wing area. With straight-lined, tapered leading and trailing edges the wings were fitted with graceful rounded tips. The tips were twisted downward a bit to prevent wingtip stall. The similarly shaped tail surfaces were generous in area to provide a high degree of maneuverability. The landing gear was of the wide tread, inward retracting type, the first "wheels up" gear ever used on a Japanese fighter. For increased range a large cylindrical drop tank was developed that hung under the forward fuselage belly.

It was a pretty aircraft and looked capable of making the designers' dreams and wishes come true. During its construction there was always a worry about the final weight coming within the limits Horikoshi knew were needed for the plane to be a success. But in the end it came within the specifications.

Another view of the captured Zero in U.S. markings, and flown by an American pilot, shows it to have extremely clean lines and superb 360-degree cockpit visibility. (National Archives)

Completion date was March 16, 1939, at Mitsubishi's Nagoya facility. Within a couple of days the engine tests were completed and the new fighter moved to the Japanese Navy's Kasumigaura Airfield for the moment of truth: a flight test. While movement of a new aircraft sounds easy using our modern-day frame of reference, it wasn't then. The prototype had to be dismantled into several sections and crated for the trip. The crates were loaded on two ox carts—that's right, *ox carts!* The Navy feared that truck transport might damage the fragile airframe. The smooth, slow ox cart was the logical choice for the thirty-mile, all-day trip on the gravel road with many turns, bumps and dips.

Once at the new location the plane was reassembled. More engine runs were made along with tests of moving parts and systems, and a general overall last-minute tweaking. The aircraft's weight and center of gravity were measured. April 1, 1939, was selected as the date for the first flight, with Mitsubishi test pilot Katsuzo Shima selected to do the honors. The whole thing went off like gang-busters and the Japanese Navy had the impossible plane it had asked for only a few months earlier. The only problems encountered were in the wheel brakes, the lubrication system and a slight tendency of the aircraft to vibrate. The first two items were simply fixed and the vibration was taken care of by going to a larger three-blade constant-speed propeller.

The Navy took over the prototype September 14, 1939. Its official title became A6M1 Carrier Fighter. Number two aircraft came along on October 18, 1939, and was accepted by the Navy a week later.

It was particularly interesting to note that the two prototypes were fitted with armament. Usually there are only provisions on prototypes for the armament to be added later—the initial flights are made without guns. These prototype Zeros packed two 20 mm cannon in the wings and two

The A6M2 was built with great attention to the power-to-weight ratio, that is, everything was built as light as possible. This attempt was successful and for a time the Japanese had the world's fastest and longest-range carrier fighter. (National Archives)

7.7 mm machine guns in the fuselage. The machine-gun barrels protruded from the upper engine cowling.

Always searching for something even better, the Navy noted that a new engine had come on the scene, the Nakajima NK1C Sakae 12 ("prosperity"). It was still a fourteen-cylinder twin-row radial but it turned out 925 horsepower. The Navy asked Mitsubishi to include the new engine as part of the number-three prototype then being built. (The third aircraft's nomenclature was updated to A6M2.) By January 18, 1940, the new, more powerful Zero was in the air and it exceeded even the most enthusiastic hopes of the Navy in the climb and speed departments.

Since everything was going so well with the new fighter the Navy decided to send a batch of them into combat for a real first-hand wringing out against the enemy. Fifteen machines were prepared for China in a hurry and they left Japan for the mainland July 21, 1940. They succeeded so well they were officially released for production; and that is when the name Zero came about. It was officially named the Type 0 Carrier Fighter (based on the last number of the Japanese year, 2600 in this case). It all took place a year and a half before Pearl Harbor but the U.S. knew nothing about the new aircraft.

Due to the surprise of seeing such a high-performance fighter sweeping the skies clean after Pearl Harbor the plane created a kind of myth in the minds of the Allies. The new machine seemed unbeatable in dogfighting. There was little question that it was the world's foremost carrier fighter during those early days of Grumman Wildcats and Brewster Buffalos. Even the Curtiss P-40's of the Flying Tigers didn't have much of a chance against them. The Zeros did so well the Japanese soon began to believe the myth of their own making. However, like all good myths, this one came to a sudden end in, of all places, the Aleutian Islands of Alaska.

It was June 3, 1942, when Flight Petty Officer Tadayoshi Koga took off in his Zero from the carrier *Ryujo*. The A6M2 had been added to an attack group scheduled to hit Dutch Harbor, an American outpost in the Aleutians. This Zero was a late model, having left the factory doors only some five months before. It was the plane's first time out in combat operations—and its last. With the attack completed, returning to the carrier, Koga found a problem that was the bane of all pilots far from their carriers: A gas tank had been holed. Since the Zero did not have a self-

This second captured Zero was sent around the country for evaluation by the nation's fighter manufacturers. This photo was taken at the Curtiss-Wright plant in Buffalo, New York. (Joseph Hofmann Collection)

sealing tank it was either down in the water or land on one of the outer Aleutians. Koga chose the latter, as the ocean in that latitude is mighty cold, even in June. The island was Aktan and had been earmarked by the Japanese as an emergency landing area in case of just such circumstances. But the Zero flipped on its back in the marsh during the landing and Koga died with a broken neck in the process. An American naval scouting party found the overturned Zero a few weeks later.

Damage to the plane was minimal and it was soon shipped back to the United States and placed in A-1 flying shape. It didn't take long for the American pilots to discover not only what a hot airplane it was but also its shortcomings. It was a real piece of luck to find the Zero intact because before that, over a six-month period, Allied Intelligence had tried to build a Zero from scraps and fragments of those destroyed in combat near enough to be recoverable. At the time of finding Koga's whole plane they had not progressed much.

It wasn't long after the evaluation of the plane, however, that word got out to the Wildcat pilots in the Pacific: Don't try to dogfight with the Zero!

What the U.S. team found in going over the captured Zero was really not all that surprising. Basically, it was a lightly built, unarmored fighter with a great ability for aerobatics. In a dogfight it was dynamite on the attack, but if it got on the receiving end of an enemy's machine-gun fire it was all over—nothing left but a flaming ball. A quick description of the fighter as seen by the Allied investigating team is interesting.

Starting at the front, there was the ten-foot three-inch Sumitomo constant-speed propeller. Its hub was faired nicely, with a two-piece streamlined spinner. Driving the propeller, by the time the A6M3 model came around, was the Nakajima Sakae 21, a fourteen-cylinder twin-row radial that put out 1,130 horsepower. The close-fitting cowl was split in two halves for easy removal with four hand-fastening clamps on either side. On the cowl's upper side were ports for two 7.7 mm aircraft machine guns and on some models there was a third 7.7 mounted beneath the skin on the left side of the fuselage just in front of the cockpit. At the rear edge of the engine cowl were manually operated cowl flaps. Just aft of the cowl's rear edge was the carburetor air scoop which hung below the forward fuselage belly. Behind it was the light firewall that was strengthened with a ring bulkhead. The engine was attached to the fuselage at this point by typical welded steel-alloy tubing connecting the engine mounting ring to the firewall, or front structural member of the fuselage. In front of the firewall was the oil tank. Between the firewall and cockpit was the forward fuselage fuel tank.

An A6M2 sports very clean lines from any view, including the underside. (Author Collection)

Moving into the cockpit it was interesting to note the canopy frame was made of aluminum and plywood, a distinct departure from normal fighter plane design practice. Typical flight and engine instruments were located on a panel in front of the pilot and the gunsight was above the panel. Engine controls were on the left cockpit wall and electrical and radio equipment on the right wall. Control of the aircraft was by a conventional stick and rudder. The cockpit seat was adjustable. And there was a high bulkhead behind the pilot's seat for rollover protection.

A few things *not* in the pilot's area, which were in most other fighter planes of the world, were self-sealing fuel tanks, armor plate for the pilot and fire protection devices. That all took up needless weight in the eyes of the Japanese Navy. The philosophy was that if the aircraft was nimble and fast enough, the pilot would not need any such trappings.

Inside the canopy, behind the rollover structure, was the directional finder loop. It was used for long-range navigation at sea.

The aircraft's structure was of semimonocoque style. The fuselage was made of fifteen nearly equally spaced cross-sectional rings held in position by twenty-four stringers. The entire assembly was then covered with sheet aluminum. Tail surfaces were of "built up" construction with all-metal formed ribs and multispars in both the vertical fin and stabilizer. The metal-framed elevators and rudder were fabric covered. The streamlined metal tail cone at the fuselage rear was lightly constructed and provided aft streamlining as well as the housing for the full-swiveling retractable tail wheel and taillight. The tail wheel gear was attached to the rearmost fuselage former ring, which was reinforced for the purpose. An arresting hook dropped from the fuselage underside in front of the tail wheel. Behind the pilot's compartment in the fuselage was the oxygen tank with its pressure gauge and regulator and the Aero Mk.3 receiver/transmitter with a radio homing device and direction finder.

The wing structure consisted of two built-up main spars of ESD. In addition to the main spars a short stub-spar extended outward for the main landing gear leg attachment. The front and rear main spars were built up of T-shaped bars with a thin aluminum web riveted between them. The final assemblies formed light, but very strong, I-beams. Twenty-four built-up ribs in each wing, covered with flush-riveted sheet aluminum alloy, gave the structure its shape. Formed wingtips completed the assembly of the basic wing. On some early models of the Zero, wingtips folded upward for carrier storage. Metal-framed slotted ailerons were fabric covered, however; the hydraulically actuated split flaps were all metal.

In the inboard sections of the wing, between the landing gear legs, were right and left main fuel tanks. The landing gear retracted inward hydraulically with half-circle wheel covers retracting outward so that the full main gear was faired smoothly into the wing's underside. The 20 mm cannon, one in each wing, were located outboard on each wing and ammunition was loaded through access panels in the wing's top surface.

When taken apart piece by piece by Allied Intelligence and pilots that flew it for evaluation, the Zero was shown to be a somewhat flimsy flying machine that was not to be overly feared. It was apparent that the dreaded Zero was a fire trap if hit by even a few slugs from the fifty-calibers the Allied fighters were capable of throwing out. The one area in which the plane was very formidable was that of maneuverability.

Yes, the Zero myth was shattered. It was not an invincible killer plane conjured up in the mysterious Far East. Only the surprise of its existence had given rise to the myth and, once known, there was little to fear of it. In fact, beating the Zero at its own game was what the Hellcat was all about.

The design tack taken by Grumman was similar to, but yet different from, the Japanese way. Grumman's advantage was in the availability of the whopping Pratt & Whitney R-2800 engine with 2,000 horsepower available. That was more than twice what the Japanese designers had access to when they designed the Zero.

As stated earlier in this chapter, the Japanese started the Zero design by first selecting an engine and proceeding as the engine's power dictated. Grumman, with twice the power of the Japanese engine, plus a leg-up on the learning curve because it knew the adversary, predictably came up with a real winner in the F6F-3.

With the Hellcats' fine performance, the tides of the Pacific war accelerated against the Japanese at an ever quickening pace. The Zeros were badly outclassed. Other Japanese fighters were designed and built in lesser numbers to counteract the Hellcat, as it had counteracted the Zero. But with the limited resources available in wartime Japan, it was impossible to produce enough of the new fighters to change the war's course by any measurable amount.

However, even though the Zero *was* just an ordinary fighter, the design went on to cause the Allies trouble of one sort or another for the remainder of the war in the Pacific. As with other fighters, the Zero was continually developed to an ever higher state of performance. It was far easier to modify an existing aircraft, as better technology became available, than it was to start over.

In the case of the Zero (of which the A6M-1, -2 and -3 models have been described), improvements continued. Here is a brief description of Zero models that followed.

With the Zero's initial acceptance by the Japanese Navy, shortly after its fine showing on mainland China, a production line was set up at the Mitsubishi Number Three airframe plant at Nagoya, home of the prototype and initial production aircraft. About this time the second Zero prototype crashed. A wing folded up during flight test due to spar failure. Redesign of the spar followed, with hopes that no more of the first twenty-one Zeros already built would have the same problem. Needless to say, the twenty-second Zero had a spar that you could drive a truck over without breaking!

Sixty-four of the initial Zeros were built and secret trials were underway to qualify them for carrier service. Previous victories in China had all been from a land base, which was different from going to sea with the much more stringent takeoff, landing and storage requirements of carrier duty. The trials consisted of testing the A6M2, or Model 11, aircraft

A lineup of Zero fighters at a Japanese airfield during World War II. As the war proceeded the design grew obsolete, despite constant attempts by the Japanese to update it. And by the time the F6F Hellcat series came along Allied pilots could defeat the Zero on a regular basis. (Author Collection)

for the rigorous duty. It didn't make the grade—the wings were too long and there were other minor, but easily corrected, defects. The outer twenty inches of each wingtip were redesigned to fold inward and the Model 11 became Model 21. It was accepted by the Navy for carrier use. Even though it was the Model 21, it was still designated the A6M2. In February 1941, a new aileron tab mechanism was perfected that assisted lowering aileron loads at high speeds.

In that form the Zero went to war at Pearl Harbor and throughout the Pacific. In early 1942 there were well over 400 Zeros ready for combat. The type was good enough that Mitsubishi eventually built 740 Model 21's before turning to later, more advanced models. Even Nakajima, which was originally skeptical of such a radical new fighter, started building the Model 21 in November 1941, a month before Pearl Harbor.

Then came a brainstorm by the Japanese Navy: How about a fighter plane on floats? It was thought that the new concept would allow fighter protection for amphibious landing parties on islands before they captured suitable bases for land-based operations. Nakajima got the contract for a production run, for it had previous experience in building float-type aircraft (as well as some pretty great flying boats).

In February 1943, the firm began work on a prototype that, based on the Zero, would meet the new design requirements. By November 1943, 327 of the float-fighters had been built. That gave the Zero, which the Allies had called Zeke, a new code name. When it was fitted with floats it was Rufe.

With a big, center float slung underneath, plus two wingtip floats, the Rufes were no great shakes as fighters. Quite a few of them got knocked down by the Wildcats and, later, Hellcats. They eventually were relegated to reconnaissance duties where they could generally stay out of trouble. They wound up in such nonactive places as Kiska and Attu in the Aleutians, and on lakes defending the home islands of Honshu and Paramushiro, neither of which were under attack in those early days of the war. Their only real victory was that Grumman and Edo wasted some time and taxpayers' money countering with a floatplane version of the Wildcat.

As the war developed, other versions of the Zero met the needs of increasing conflict. A two-seat trainer version of the Zero was next. Even the invincible Japanese needed a good way to train invincible pilots to fly invincible Zeros in combat. That aircraft was labeled the 17-Shi Fighter

Trainer. Even though a larger canopy was fitted to house the instructor, the student pilot had to sit out in the airstream behind an open-cockpit windshield. Another result of the modification was the addition of small fins on either side of the fuselage; they made the aircraft stable in spite of the oversized canopy. The armament carried on the trainer was cut down to two 7.7 mm machine guns. The top speed fell off to 296 miles per hour at about 13,000 feet.

As was the case with fighter development the world over, the Zero acquired still larger engines, horsepower-wise, and the speed and performance increased. The plane was modified again and again in hopes of keeping up with the new Allied aircraft, particularly the Hellcat.

The A6M3 got a bigger engine, a 1,130-horsepower Sakae 21. It was fitted with a two-speed supercharger and, when opened up, could move the new-model Zero along at 341 miles per hour at 20,500 feet. With this model the designers also clipped the wings and removed the aileron tab balances. That was in September 1942, and the Allies were still somewhat spooked over new Japanese fighter aircraft. When the square-winged Zero was sighted in action over Guadalcanal the Allies figured it was something completely new. They were quick to nickname it the Hap; but changed it to Hamp in deference to "Hap" Arnold. And all the while, it was only a Zeke with clipped wings! The clipped wing didn't help maneuverability, but in a dive, the smaller wing area did increase speed. After several hundred were built the rounded, folding wingtips were again added to the design.

Other models followed, each a definite improvement over the previous; each one's design an attempt to catch up with the now rampaging Hellcats. Guns were added, wingspan was changed, and anything else that could be thought of was done to make the aircraft an even better fighting machine.

The final missions for the Zero, which had over the war years become ever more obsolete, were the suicide ones. They were the kamikaze planes that, for a period, did serious damage to the U.S. surface fleet. Zeros making up Air Group 201 in the Philippines were the first to actually undertake a mission in which self-destruction was assured. It was manned by all-volunteer airmen. The Zeros were outfitted with heavy bombs, as there was no purpose in using up the aircraft's gross takeoff weight with fuel for a return flight home.

The initial success led to the formation of more kamikaze units. The Zero, the scourge of Chinese skies in pre-Pearl Harbor days, was now relegated to the torturous death march of a panic-stricken Japanese nation fighting for mere survival. The Zero hour had ended.

INSIDE A HELLCAT

CHAPTER VI

The F6F Hellcat was a Wildcat descendant, stretched and modernized beyond recognition to handle the big Pratt & Whitney R-2800 engine—the same engine that made the P-47 Thunderbolt, F4U Corsair and B-26 Marauder aircraft so great. The plane was unmistakably Grumman. The fuselage had been lengthened to provide a longer tail moment to counteract the torque of the powerful Double Wasp. With the longer fuselage came a larger squared-off wing. The Wildcat mid-wing was changed to a low-wing position to accommodate the wing-mounted retract gear. The hand-cranked, chain-driven fuselage-flank-style landing gear Grumman had used for well over a decade was now obsolete. The major drawback to the old method was the narrow tread between the main wheels that made ground-looping easy with the Wildcat (and would have been a certainty with the 2,000-horsepower Hellcat). The new landing gear retracted rearward and rotated ninety degrees to lie flat against the rear underportion of the wing, just as on the Curtiss P-40 and the later F4U Corsair.

A walk around the new "cat" revealed a powerful, no frills, down-to-earth combat machine that was rugged in construction and had a simplistic beauty all its own.

Starting at the very front of the aircraft there was the thirteen-foot-one-inch-diameter Hamilton Standard Hydromatic three-blade propeller. It was a constant-speed unit, doing the same job the Curtiss Electric had on the Wildcat—full horsepower delivered regardless of airspeed and rpm. The prop was large, with only a little over seven inches of ground clearance when the tail was up in the takeoff position and the landing gear oleos depressed by the weight of the aircraft. Not exactly great for taxiing through stumps but perfectly satisfactory for use on smooth-surfaced carrier decks.

The big prop was required to absorb the whopping 2,000 horsepower put out by the Pratt & Whitney R-2800-10W engine, an eighteen-cylinder air-cooled radial machine of jewellike precision. The centerline of the engine was slanted downward at an angle of three degrees. That gave the aircraft, from the side view, the head-down appearance of a charging bull. The real purpose of the head-down appearance was to keep the wing relation to the fuselage with a minimum amount of incidence for the least drag possible in level flight. Since a large angle of attack was required in relation to the engine thrust line, the engine was tilted downward, which resulted in a slight tail-down flight attitude. A spinoff of the arrangement was increased forward visibility for the pilot when looking over the nose of the aircraft.

The R-2800-10 engine was an evolutionary development of the earlier R-1830 series. With a displacement of 2800 cubic inches (that's 155

This photo, released September 9, 1943, shows off to the public one of the early production F6F-3 Hellcats. It was the first new American warplane design that was based on combat experience gained during World War II. (U.S. Navy)

cubic inches *per cylinder!*), the Double Wasp incorporated two blower units: main and auxiliary. The main stage turned at a fixed ratio to engine crankshaft speed. The auxiliary stage could be either completely disengaged from the crankshaft or, by means of hydraulic cone clutches, shifted to either low- or high-blower ratios. The arrangement's extra boost at high altitude really paid off in increased performance.

The propeller reduction ratio was .5 to 1, that is, the propeller turned at half the crankshaft speed. That allowed for large-diameter propeller blades while still keeping the blade tips below supersonic speed. Gearing for the reduction was in the crankcase nose.

The rear engine case was large and extended well back from the twin rows of cylinders. It housed the supercharger impellers, their clutches and gearing. Other items in the case included the generator drive, tachometer drive, hydraulic and vacuum pumps, the starter drive and the oil inlet and outlet fittings and filters. Underneath the case was slung a big three-barrel carburetor. The massive crankshaft was supported by steel-backed bronze bearings located in the front, middle and rear crankcase sections. The engine weighed about 2,500 pounds.

The engines were complex and, aside from regular maintenance, were not all that easy to repair aboard ship. As the war came nearer its end it was not too unusual for a broken engine, along with the attached Hellcat, to be pushed over the side rather than repaired. By then, replacement aircraft stored at island depots were readily available and could be flown out to the carriers on very short notice. While that sounds like a terrible waste, war *is* waste. In the heat of combat it is important that all equipment be up to snuff and ready to go rather than sitting unusable in a repair bay.

The engine lubrication system was of extreme importance for its successful operation. Oil does at least five things for an engine: It reduces friction, cools, cleans, acts as a seal and is a preservative. In the case of the R-2800, the oil was located in a twenty-one-gallon tank above the engine

Forward view of the F6F Hellcat instrument panel. (Grumman)

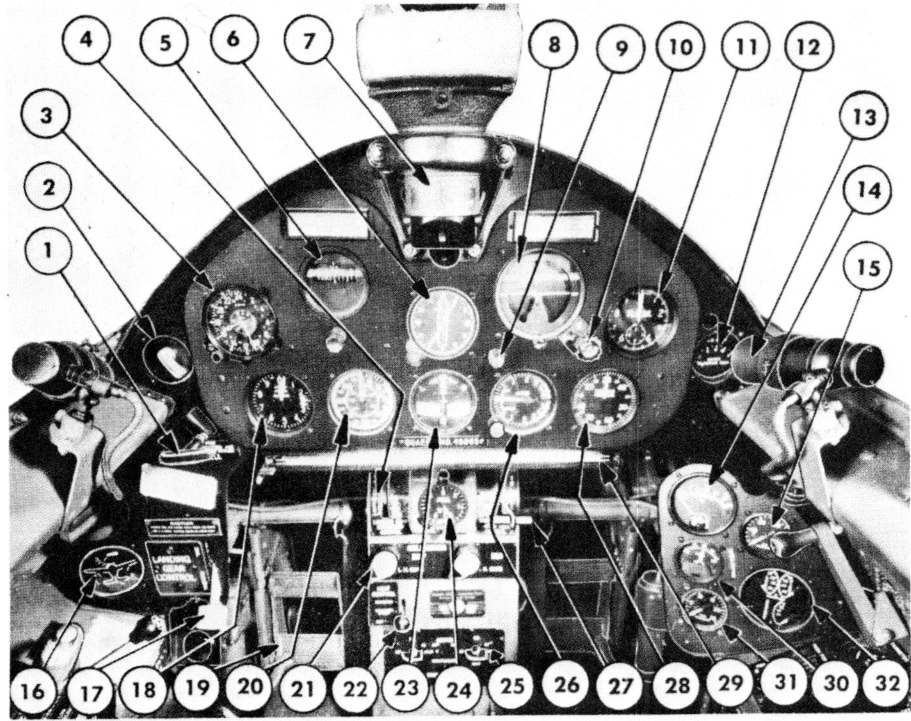

1. Carburetor Protected Air Control (Aux. Stage Only)
2. Ignition Switch
3. Clock
4. Landing Gear Emergency Lowering Control
5. Directional Gyro
6. Compass
7. Gunsight
8. Attitude Gyro
9. Chartboard Light
10. Attitude Gyro Caging Knob
11. Tachometer
12. Water Quantity Gage—A.D.I. System
13. Instrument Panel Fluorescent Light
14. Cylinder Head Temperature Gage
15. Oil Pressure Gage
16. Landing Gear & Wing Flap Position Indicator
17. Landing Gear Control
18. Altimeter
19. Rudder Pedals
20. Airspeed Indicator
21. Gun Charging Controls
22. Cockpit Heater Control
23. Turn and Bank Indicator
24. Ammunition Rounds Counter
25. Fluorescent Lights Control
26. Rate of Climb Indicator
27. Wing Lock Safety Control Handle
28. Manifold Pressure Gage
29. Chartboard
30. Oil-In Temperaure Gage
31. Fuel Pressure Gage
32. Fuel Quantity Gages

rear crankcase; however, it was only filled to about nineteen gallons to allow foaming space. The oil was circulated in the engine by a gear-type pressure pump through three branches. The first branch lubricated the crankpins, master rod bearings, floating knuckle pins, crankshaft main bearings, cylinder walls and piston pins. The second branch handled the two main impeller intermediate gears, the valve operating mechanism for the rear row of cylinders and the rear secondary counterbalance intermediate gear. The third branch lubricated the forward reduction gears, the magnetos and distributor-gear train bearings, the front counterbalance intermediate gear bearings and the front cylinder valve operating mechanism. The oil was scavenged from the engine by two separate gear pumps. The oil then went to the engine-oil cooler and back to the tank for another circuit through the engine's lubrication system.

With such a complex piece of machinery, a mechanic's preflight check was almost always undertaken before taking off. Performance was important. Like a doctor's miniphysical, a lot could be rapidly determined by an experienced hand. Here is a list of some of the steps in such a check: Inspect propeller blades for cracks, nicks and splits. Remove the engine cowling and inspect each piece for cracks (vibration sometimes had a way of making cracks show up unexpectedly). Check the cowl flaps and make

View of F6F cockpit showing main instrumentation and controls of both the instrument panel and the left and right pilot consoles. (Grumman)

sure the snap fasteners are secure. Inspect exhaust stacks looking for cracks in the pipes and make sure the stacks are firmly attached. Check rocker box fittings, noting the caps are securely in place and there is no leakage. Check spark plug terminal assemblies for tightness and cleanliness. Check the ignition wiring and harness to be sure they are secure and not frayed. Clean the main fuel-line strainer and check out the cause of any water or dirt found in it. Look for leaks in the fuel and oil lines. (They could be easily recognized as the oil lines had a yellow band on each side of every connection. Fuel lines had a red band.) Check the tightness of the oil drain plugs and the supply of fluid in the hydraulic system reservoir. Replace the cowling, making certain it is secure. The last items checked were the amount of fuel in the tanks; the tank vents, to be sure they were open; and the oil tank, which needed to be full. The plane, enginewise at least, was then ready for takeoff.

While the oil system represented the engine circulatory innards, the fuel system made up the engine's digestive tract—and what an appetite. The system consisted of two main fuel cells located left and right of the wing center-section centerline. A reserve cell was located under the pilot's seat. The wing tanks held 87.5 gallons each and the reserve tank held 75 gallons. A centerline fuselage drop tank could hold an extra 150

The F6F left pilot console contained, among other items, the throttle, landing and cowl flap controls, trim tab controls and propeller pitch controls. (Grumman)

gallons of Grade 100/130 gasoline used in the aircraft. If the 400 gallons of fuel in those tanks was not enough, two additional 100-gallon drop tanks could be attached to the 1,000-pound bomb racks under the wing center section. Selection of the tank to draw from was by means of a selector valve located in the cockpit. To prevent the pilot from unknowingly running out of fuel, a reserve tank warning light was located on the fuel control panel and would glow when the reserve tank was down to fifty gallons or less. That meant he really ought to be heading back to base!

The engine was mounted to the airframe with a typical engine-mounting ring attached to the engine just behind the back row of cylinders. The attachment was with Lord rubber bushings to isolate the airframe from engine vibrations. Welded high-strength alloy steel tub legs tied the mounting ring to the airframe at the stainless steel firewall. Forward of the firewall was the oil tank and its armor plating, the engine accessories and the engine-oil cooler ductwork. Engine cowling and removable sheet metal panels covered the area from the firewall to the engine cowl nose ring. The cowl flaps were located on the upper trailing edge of the cowling and were pilot controlled.

From the firewall aft, the fuselage was all-metal semi-monocoque construction consisting of twenty-one formers and bulkheads to define the fuselage cross-sectional shape. They were connected in the longitu-

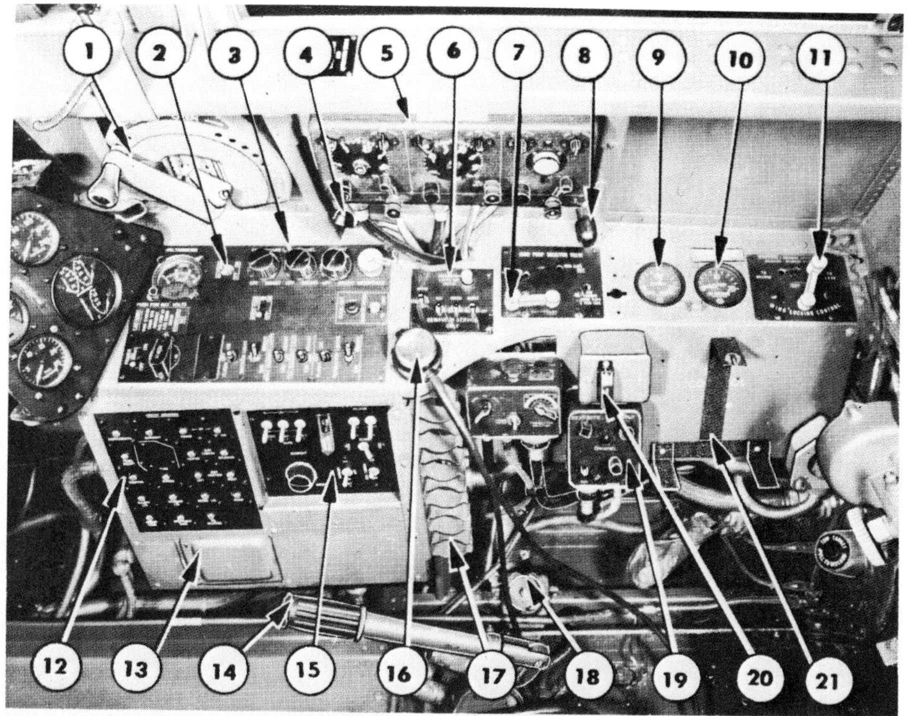

1. Cabin Sliding Hood Control
2. Battery Switch
3. Main Electrical Distribution Panel
4. Electrical Panel Light
5. Radio Controls
6. Recognition Lights
7. Hand Pump Selector Valve
8. Aft Right Cockpit Shelf Light
9. Hydraulic System Pressure Gage
10. Landing Gear Emergency Dump Pressure Gage
11. Wing Locking Hydraulic Control
12. Manual Reset Circuit Breaker Panel
13. Access to Reverse Current Relay
14. Hydraulic Hand Pump
15. Armament Panel
16. Hand Microphone
17. Pyrotechnic Cartridge Clips
18. Pyrotechnic Pistol Retainer
19. Radio Controls
20. IFF Destruction Switch
21. IFF Equipment Support

The F6F right pilot console was given over primarily to communication and electrical system controls. (Grumman)

dinal direction by twenty stringers or longerons. At each joint between the formers and stringers was a riveted gusset. The construction made an extremely strong, though light, framework to which formed aluminum sheet covering was flush riveted. In the cockpit area the structure was heavily reinforced. To further protect the pilot, armor plate was located both in front of the instrument panel and as a bulkhead at the rear of the cockpit. On the underside of the cockpit the self-sealing fuel tanks gave a secondary degree of pilot protection.

Since the Hellcat was a relatively large aircraft, the cockpit was roomy by fighter plane standards. The canopy was made up of Plexiglas with a sturdy metal frame. It slid rearward on tracks in the conventional manner. An external release button was located on the right side of the fuselage just below the windshield frame. After pushing the button the canopy could easily be slid to the open position. From the inside, the pilot, using a handcrank located on the right cockpit wall, could crank counterclockwise to close the canopy and clockwise to open it. A series of holes in a fixed plate behind the crank accepted a pin mounted on the crank so that the canopy could be locked in any degree of opening the pilot chose. It took about 4½ revolutions to run the canopy full travel in either direction. To get a quick release during emergencies, the pilot pulled two red rings that were attached to latches located at the forward end of the canopy track. Once released, the canopy blew away in the airstream.

Seven F6F-3's during a training flight near San Diego on September 9, 1943. E markings are white and the craft are possibly from VF-18. (National Archives)

The windshield assembly was made of a bullet-resistant glass front plate with Plexiglas panels on either side and at the top. It was held together with a sturdy aluminum frame. A lever on the lower center control panel could direct a flow of warm air on the windshield for defrosting. Actually the level did more than that, for it was a foot-warmer control too. Moved upward it defrosted the windshield, in the center position it defrosted the windshield and warmed the pilot's feet, and moved downward it was for feet only.

Once in the cockpit the pilot's attention was first given to getting the seat set up so that he could see well outside the aircraft, read the instruments easily and, most of all, feel comfortable. On a several-hour mission, that was important. The control lever for vertical seat adjustment was located on the seat's right side. With it, the seat could be moved about six inches up and down full travel, enough to take care of just about anyone. On the left side of the seat was the lever for adjustment of the shoulder straps, which incidentally had to be over a structural cross-bar in the rear of the cockpit.

Grumman F6F-3
Hellcat

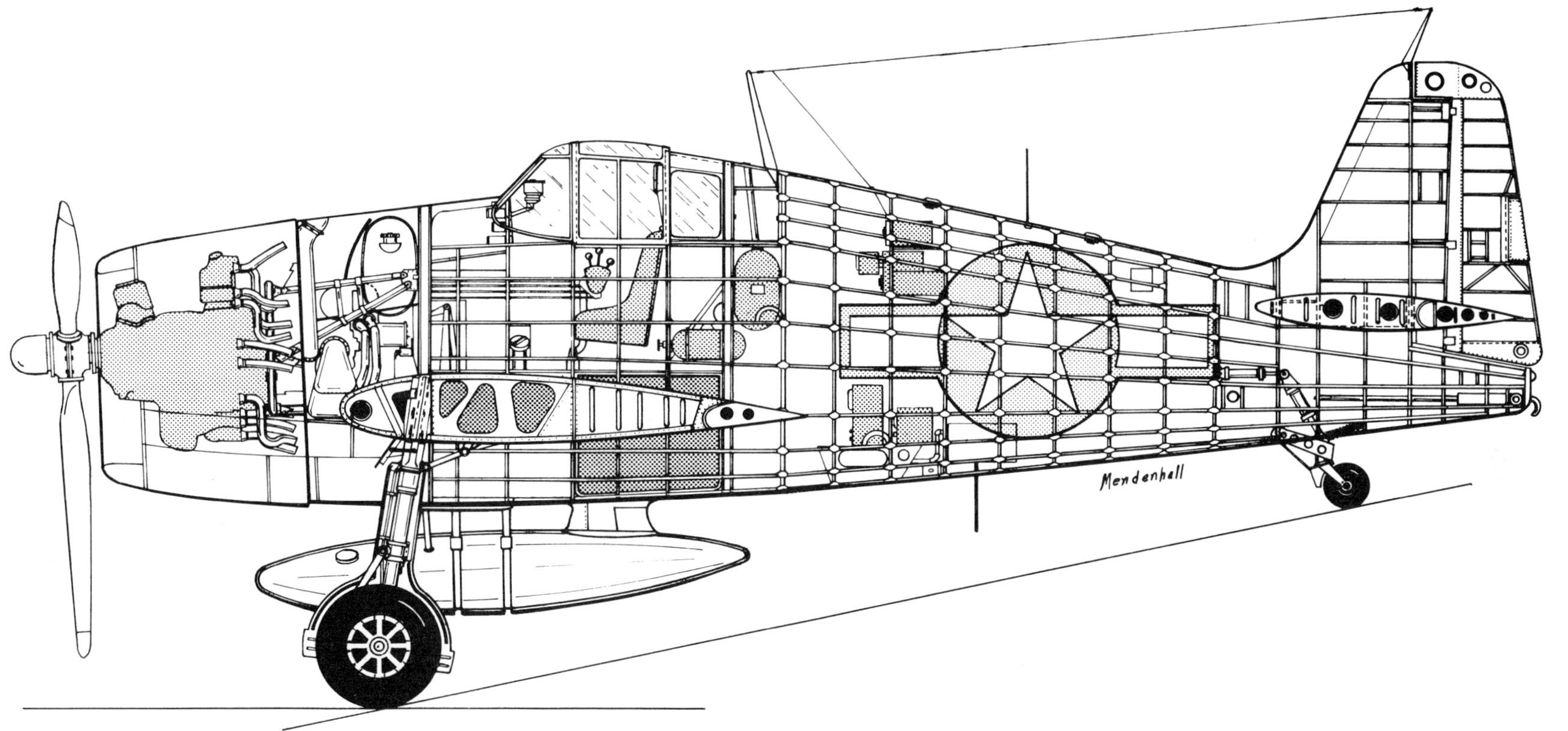

inboard profile

Hellcat drop tanks are being manhandled about the deck of the carrier USS *Bunker Hill.* The aircraft are VF-8 F6F-3's and were marked with black cowl numbers. As can be seen, the lower cowl flaps have been eliminated and a bulge over the central exhaust system is present. Photo was taken in June 1944. (National Archives)

Strapped in and ready to go, the pilot would be needing oxygen once he got to the usual combat altitude. A 514-cubic-inch shatterproof bottle charged to 1,800 psi took care of that supply. The bottle, located behind the pilot's seat, was fitted with a regulator to bring the pressure to a breathable level. The extended control knob for the regulator was located to the left of the pilot's seat, as was the breathing tube and facepiece.

Directly in front of the pilot was the main instrument panel containing flight, navigation and engine instruments. The flight instruments consisted of the usual altimeter, airspeed indicator, turn and bank indicator and rate-of-climb indicator. The navigation instruments were just as conventional: clock, directional gyro, compass, artificial horizon indicator, caging knob and a chart board with light. Engine instruments were the carburetor-protected air control, ignition switch tachometer, water quantity gauge (for the antidetonation system), cylinder head temperature gauge, oil pressure gauge, oil temperature gauge, manifold pressure gauge, fuel pressure gauge and fuel quantity gauges.

With those basics accounted for, there were still more controls to be reckoned with on the forward panel: landing gear emergency-lowering control, electric gun sight, instrument panel light, landing gear and wing flap position indicator, landing gear control, gun charging controls, cockpit heater control, ammunition rounds counter, wing lock safety control handle and, if the pilot glanced beneath the panel, on the floor, the rudder pedals that were adjustable to his leg length. Nothing in a fighter plane is as simple as the above, however. There were panel consoles on either side of the pilot as well.

The left side of the cockpit was devoted to engine-related controls that could not be placed on the forward instrument panel. The right-side console contained items mainly of an electrical nature. The arrangement was very similar to, but more sophisticated than, that previously described for the Wildcat's cockpit.

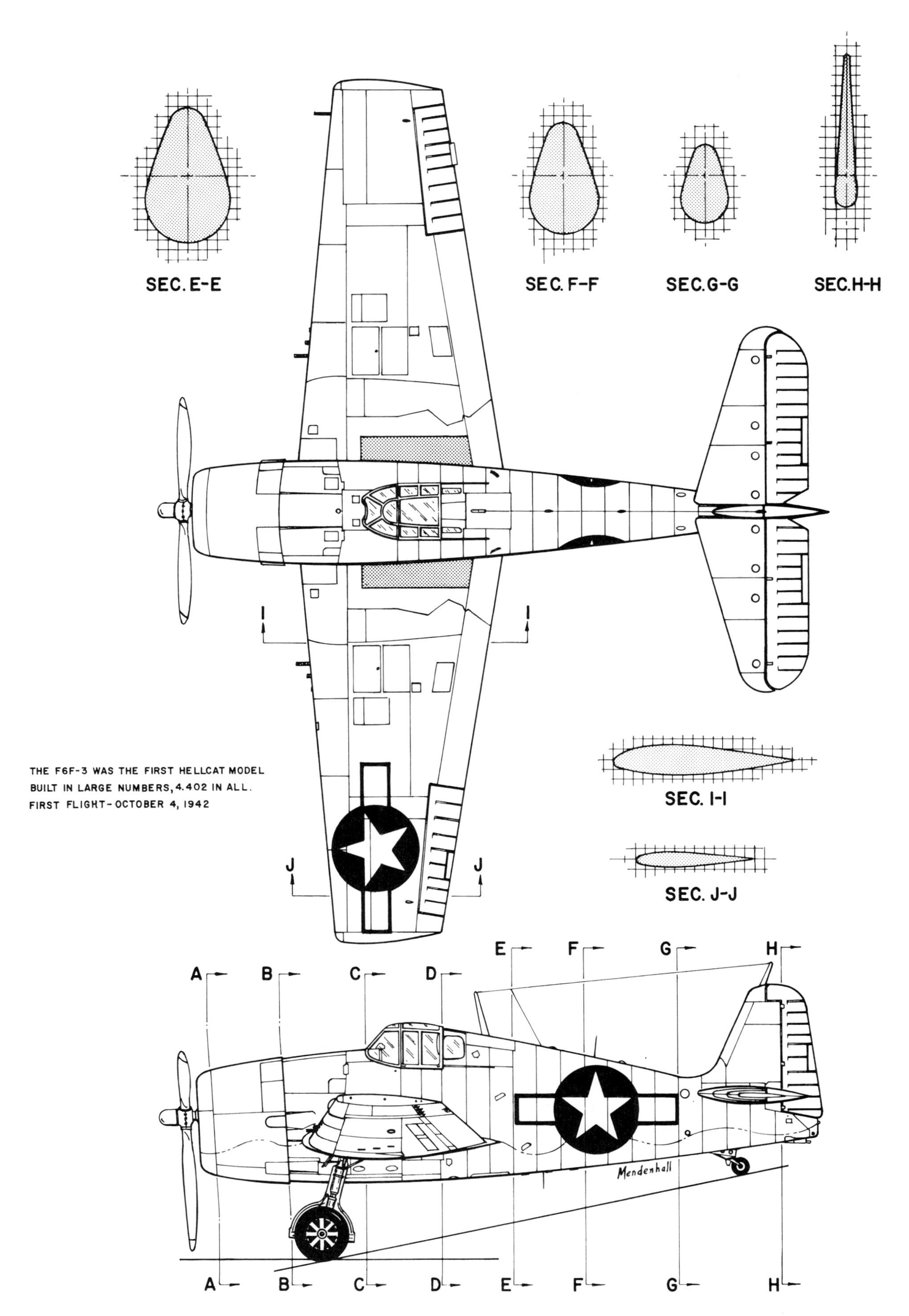
SEC. E-E
SEC. F-F
SEC. G-G
SEC. H-H
THE F6F-3 WAS THE FIRST HELLCAT MODEL
BUILT IN LARGE NUMBERS, 4.402 IN ALL.
FIRST FLIGHT - OCTOBER 4, 1942
SEC. I-I
SEC. J-J
A
B
C
D
E
F
G
H
I
J
Mendenhall

This F6F-5 obviously went off the deck during a landing attempt. Note the extended arresting hook with no deck cable attached. (National Air & Space Museum)

The left side of the cockpit, in detail, contained engine controls for the cowl flap, oil cooler and intercooler shutter, throttle, mixture, supercharger, antidetonation system, auxiliary electric fuel pump, fuel tank pressure, propeller pitch, and fuel tank selector valve and reserve fuel tank warning light. Flight controls situated on the left cockpit side included the rudder trim tab control, wing flap electrical switch, flap manual control and the elevator and aileron trim tab controls. The other items located on the cockpit left side were such things as cockpit lights, tail wheel lock control, mask microphone switch and map case.

The right side of the cockpit, as mentioned, contained the electrical and radio systems. Here was the main electrical distribution panel, battery switch, radio controls, recognition lights, machine gun switches, bomb control switches, radio destruction switch, hand microphone, gunsight rheostat and switch, IFF equipment support and recognition lights. Some controls of the hydraulic system were also found on the right side of the cockpit, such as the wing-locking hydraulic control, hand pump selec-

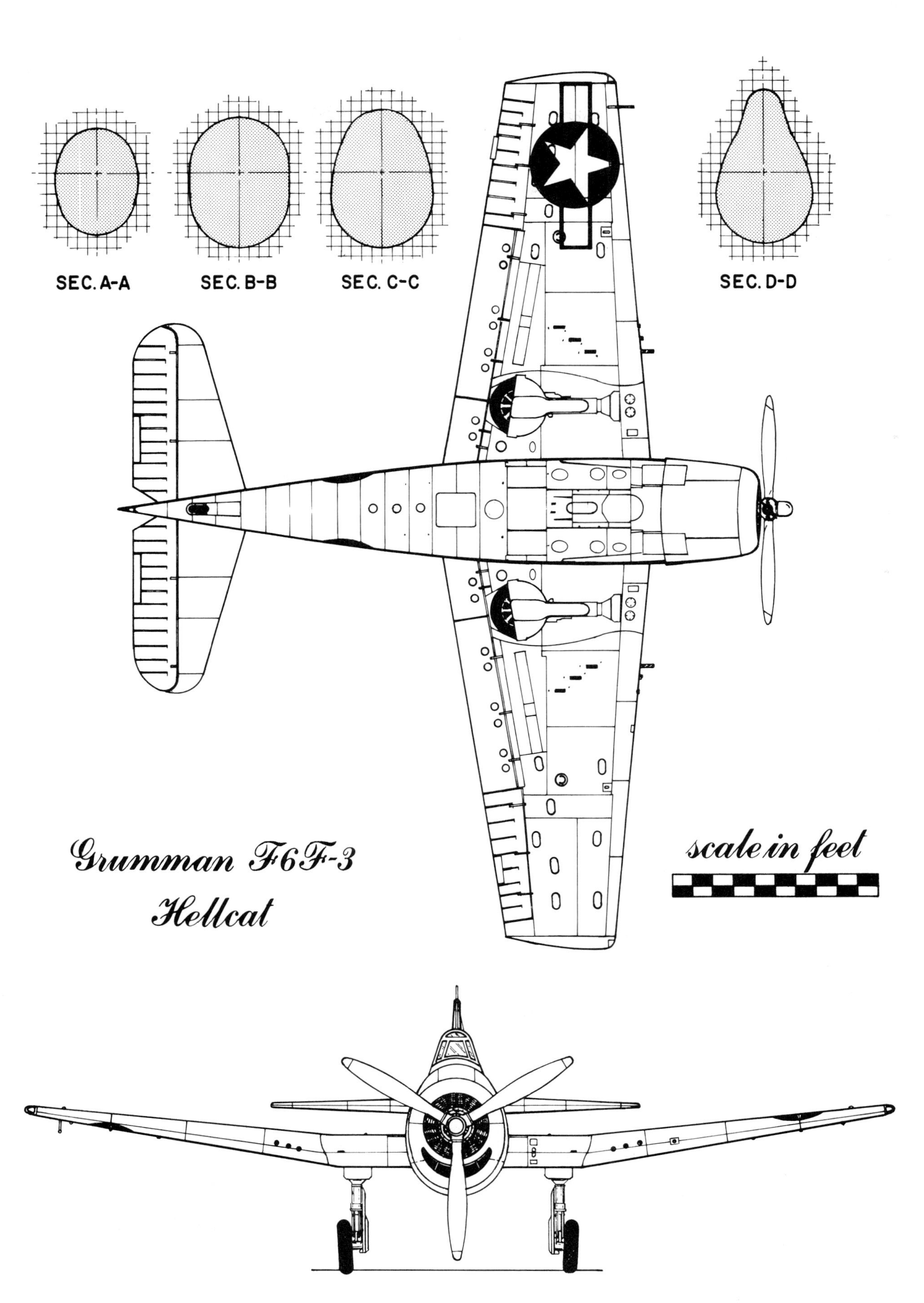
SEC. A-A
SEC. B-B
SEC. C-C
SEC. D-D
Grumman F6F-3
Hellcat
scale in feet

tor valve, hydraulic hand pump (used if the engine-driven pump failed), hydraulic system pressure gauge, and landing gear emergency dump pressure gauge. Located here also was a pyrotechnic pistol with cartridges.

Behind the seat were located the oxygen tank supply control valve, an arresting hook emergency control handle, an IFF receptacle and a tow-target release control.

While most of these instruments and controls are typical and similar to those of the Wildcat, there were certain exclusive features that will be covered in more detail.

The Bendix Fuel Pressurization System was operated by a push-pull T-handle located on the fuel control panel. It was used at altitudes over 12,000 feet for economical cruising where the auxiliary electric fuel pump was not as efficient or effective. In combat it was disengaged for fear a bullet hole in a tank could result in fuel being forced from the tank under pressure before the self-sealing latex could plug it. However, for the flight home, that was not really a problem as the tank would seal itself after about one minute. The auxiliary electric pump was also used while starting the engine, when shifting from one fuel tank to another, or at any other time when it was required to maintain the steady fuel pressure needed for good engine performance.

Wing folding, while not controlled from the cockpit (wings were spread and folded manually), was locked and unlocked from the cockpit. That control was via a T-handle located on the lower center instrument panel that operated the safety mechanism for the hydraulically operated main locking pins. A two-position lever valve located on the right-hand console actually controlled the locking pin movement. The purpose of the safety system was to prevent the main locking pins from unlocking during flight regardless of what happened to the plane's hydraulic system.

This is how the system worked: After landing, the first step was to make sure the wing flaps were up. The next step was to disengage the safety lock pins by pushing the T-handle left and full-up. Next the lever for the hydraulic locking pin valve was pushed to the fold position. If the engine was not running, the hand pump would have to be used to activate the locking pins. The wing panels were then manually pushed back along the fuselage sides until the "folded" lock pin was engaged. As a safety measure, since the distance between the wing and the fuselage sides was small, it was a good idea to keep any part of the body inside the cockpit during the folding operation.

To spread the Hellcat's wings, if the engine was not running, the hydraulic system had to be hand pumped up to about 1,500 psi. The wings were then manually pushed out to the spread position and the charged system would insert the locking pins. A few extra strokes were pumped to make sure the pins were fully in place. The T-handle was then pushed full-down and right, to engage the safety lock. The wings were checked to make sure red "unlocked" warning flags were down and flush on each wing. They signified that the wings were fully locked in the spread position. Manual spreading of the wings did require care on the part of the ground crew to make sure the wing did not *fall* into the spread position, which could damage the wing-folding mechanism.

The hydraulic locking pins for the wings were but one small part of the aircraft's hydraulic system. It also operated the wing flaps, cowl flaps, landing gear retraction (both main-gear and tail-wheel), intercooler and oil cooler shutters, and the gun-charging mechanism. (Those systems were handled by means of mechanical cables in the case of the Wildcat, save for the pneumatically operated flaps.) The hydraulic system used 1.7 gallons of AN-VV-366 fluid, a red-colored liquid. If a pilot saw it dribbling away across the wing or cowl he knew he probably had some real problems ahead.

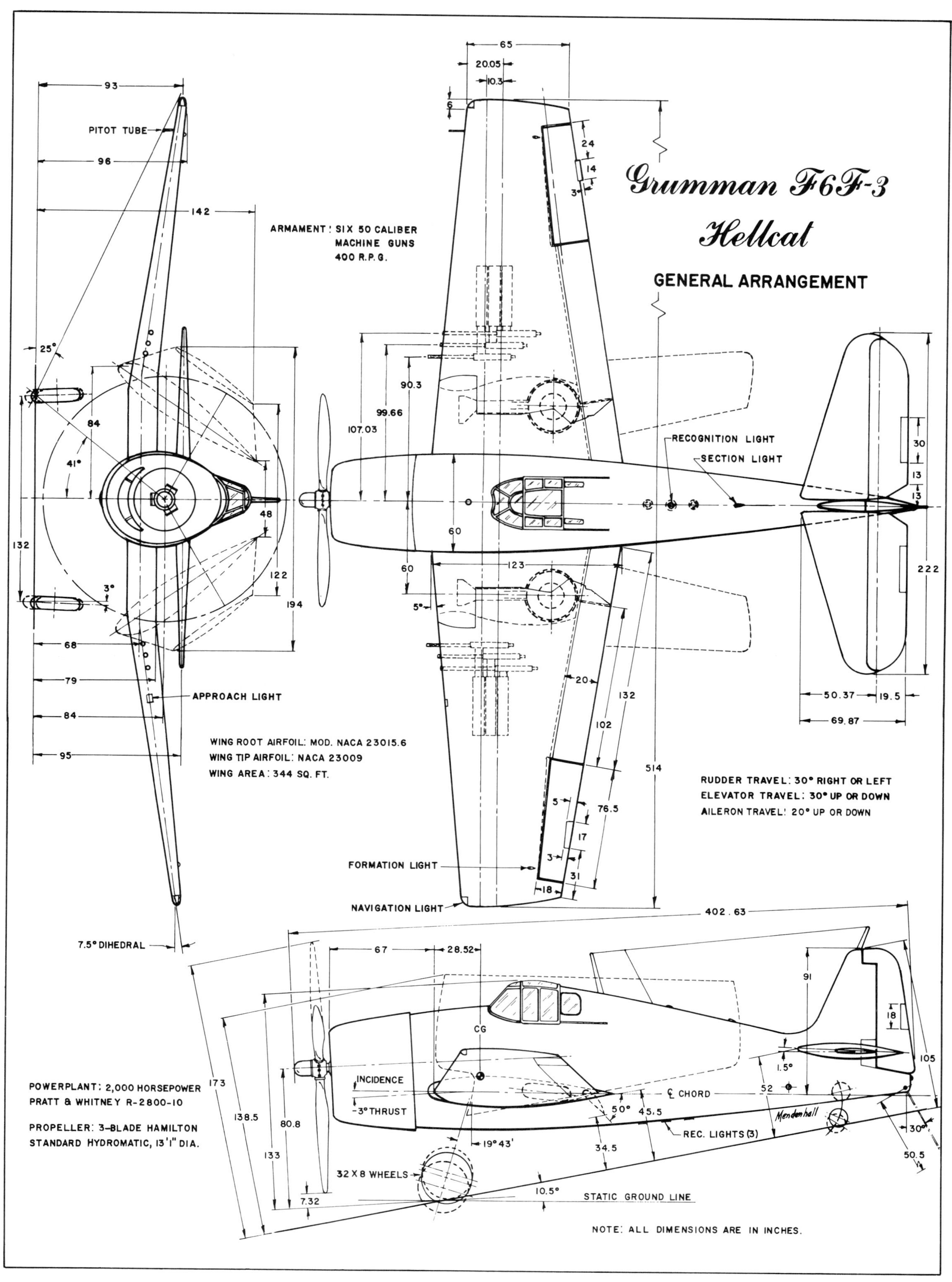

Grumman F6F-3
Hellcat
GENERAL ARRANGEMENT
ARMAMENT: SIX 50 CALIBER MACHINE GUNS 400 R.P.G.
PITOT TUBE
APPROACH LIGHT
7.5° DIHEDRAL
WING ROOT AIRFOIL: MOD. NACA 23015.6
WING TIP AIRFOIL: NACA 23009
WING AREA: 344 SQ. FT.
RECOGNITION LIGHT
SECTION LIGHT
FORMATION LIGHT
NAVIGATION LIGHT
RUDDER TRAVEL: 30° RIGHT OR LEFT
ELEVATOR TRAVEL: 30° UP OR DOWN
AILERON TRAVEL: 20° UP OR DOWN
CG
INCIDENCE
-3° THRUST
℄ CHORD
REC. LIGHTS (3)
32 X 8 WHEELS
STATIC GROUND LINE
POWERPLANT: 2,000 HORSEPOWER PRATT & WHITNEY R-2800-10
PROPELLER: 3-BLADE HAMILTON STANDARD HYDROMATIC, 13'1" DIA.
NOTE: ALL DIMENSIONS ARE IN INCHES.
Mendenhall

The mass confusion of takeoff operations aboard a carrier is shown here. The engines of many of the aircraft are running while number one, with wings unfolded, gets ready to roll. (National Air & Space Museum)

In the event of a complete hydraulic system failure the landing gear could still be extended manually. The landing gear emergency release T-handle was located on the lower center instrument panel. When the plane's speed dropped below 90 knots on approach, the handle was pushed to the full-down and locked position. That released the gear-up locks, opened a 1,950-psi bottle of compressed air into the gear hydraulic system and opened the hydraulic pump valve. In about ten seconds the gear would be down and locked.

The reason for the airspeed of 90 knots or less was that the air stored in the bottle did not have enough pressure to overcome the slipstream and the gear would only partially come down, in a trailing position. Even with the engine (or hand pump) hydraulic system in good shape the gear would not lower completely at over 135 knots. Normal operation of the landing gear was accomplished by simply moving a square-knobbed lever at the left-hand instrument panel to an "up" position for gear retraction and to a "down" position for gear extension. The square knob was used to make it different from all others by sight and feel to prevent inadvertent operation while in flight.

The four-piece wing flaps were operated by four hydraulic cylinders. The cylinders were fed by a hydraulic valve that was controlled electrically with a servo-motor. The motor was operated with a toggle switch on the left cockpit console. Pushing the switch forward brought the flaps up, and rearward extended them. If the electrical system went out, there was still a wing-flap manual control lever on the lower left side of the cockpit—not as easy to use as the switch, but still workable. If the normal hydraulic system failed, there was the auxiliary hand pump to get pressure up. If that system didn't work either, how about a no-flaps landing?

At speeds over 170 knots the flaps would not come down. The airstream presented too much pressure on them for extension. If they were not retracted as the plane accelerated past 170 knots they would automatically retract. That action was controlled by an airspeed switch connected in parallel to the airspeed indicator. If the cockpit switch was left in the "down" position the flaps would once again extend when the airspeed dropped below 170 knots.

The control stick was somewhat conventional. It was provided with a pistol-type grip and equipped with a gun trigger and bomb release button. The rudder pedals were suspended from a horizontal bar below the instrument panel. They were adjustable to any of four positions, aft or forward, by pushing the adjustment levers with the toes. The brake pedals were automatically positioned at the same time.

A more detailed look at the pilot's electrical distribution panel reveals a veritable hardware store of switches, rheostats and circuit breakers. With the Hellcat the electrical age had arrived! There were switches for running, section, tail and formation lights. There were bomb selector and bomb fusing switches, gun selector switches, gunsight, gun camera and gun master switches. The arresting hook and pitot tube heater switches, engine primer, starter cartridge firing and battery switches were also there. Rheostats controlled the intensity of the chart board light, the electrical panel, the cockpit lights and the gunsight. Circuit breakers were present for radios, lights, instruments, compass, arresting hook, droppable tank, gun heaters and the cockpit heater.

The gunsight used to aim the six fifty-caliber machine guns in the wings was located on the aircraft's centerline just above the main instrument panel. It was the Mark 8 electric type. A two-filament lamp within the sight illuminated and projected the cross hairs and deflection rings on the windshield for aiming the guns. Its rheostat controlled the light's intensity.

The radio equipment was located in the fuselage behind the cockpit. Most of its controls were on the right cockpit console. The equipment consisted of a VHF (very high frequency) receiver, HF (high frequency) receiver and navigation receiver, all of which could normally be in operation simultaneously. A microphone and headset were the pilot's interface with the equipment. The transmitting side of the equipment was the VHF transmitter and the HF transmitter. The equipment was to be explosively destroyed if there was danger of it falling in enemy hands. There was a cockpit switch to trigger the explosion.

One other piece of electronic equipment found on some Hellcats (F6F-3E and -5N) was radar, a then relatively new device that allowed night-fighter pilots to "see" an enemy in the dark. Compared to today's ultrasophisticated all-weather systems, it was pretty anemic, but every new technology has to start somewhere. The receiver and transmission equipment were located in the fuselage. The radar antenna was located in a pod either slung under (-3E) or faired into (-5N) the right wingtip. Controls for the radar were located on the left side of the cockpit, just above the engine control quadrant. The simple viewing screen was located on the centerline of the main instrument panel.

A water-injection system was installed on the Hellcat to provide what was called war-emergency-power. It was to be used only under the

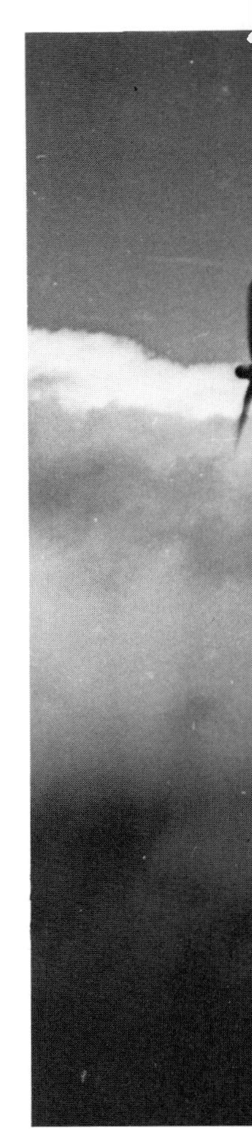

Two very nice formation pictures of Hellcats in their element with bright blue skies above and fleecy cumulus clouds below. (National Archives)

most dire conditions, since there was always the possibility of ruining the engine by its application. Continuous operation of this system was not to exceed five minutes. Application of war-emergency-power was accomplished by advancing the throttle from its normal limit stop to a full-forward position.

At the rear of the fuselage was a conventional fin/rudder vertical tail and elevator/stabilizer horizontal tail. In both cases the forward section, or fin and stabilizer, was all metal and the rudder and elevator were metal frames with fabric covering. The vertical fin was made up of two vertical spars and a tailpost located at the hinge line. Seven aluminum symmetrical ribs completed the structure which was then covered with flush-riveted aluminum alloy sheet. The vertical fin was built as an integral part of the rear fuselage. The rudder attached to it with three forged inset hinges. The rudder framework was built up of a formed aluminum tip, ten horizontal formed aluminum ribs, a formed sheet aluminum leading edge and a thin "V" trailing edge. An all-metal trim tab was inset in the rudder's trailing edge. It was controlled by a knob located on the left cockpit console. The rudder was cable operated from the cockpit by the rudder pedals. All control cables were stainless steel and double, in case one was shot away.

The horizontal tail surfaces spanned eighteen feet six inches with an overall chord of 69.87 inches. The airfoil was symmetrical, set at an incidence of 4.5 degrees relative to the thrust line. Structure of the elevator consisted of a main spar located at the hinge line with fourteen

formed aluminum ribs (per side), providing the airfoil shape. A formed aluminum leading edge was flush riveted to the ribs. The framework was then covered with formed sheet aluminum flush riveted to the structure forming a light but very strong monocoque assembly.

The elevators were made of a formed leading edge of aluminum attached to the trailing edge with thirteen (per elevator) formed ribs. A formed aluminum tip finished off the structure. Three forged inset hinges made up the attachment points of each elevator to the stabilizer. The elevator halves were covered with fabric that was stitched and taped to the ribs. The reason for fabric covering the control surfaces was to allow the pilot a "sense of feel" that went back to the days when entire aircraft were fabric covered. Metal-covered control surfaces gave too hard and abrupt a feel for pilots' liking. When jets came along and the surfaces became all metal, in spite of the pilots, an "artificial feel," simulating fabric-covered surfaces, was devised.

Inset in the trailing edge of the elevators were sheet metal trim tabs controlled by a small wheel on the left cockpit console. It was important that the elevators be in a neutral position during a catapult launch. There was at least one case in which they were not and the elevators were driven to a full-up position at launch. The aircraft went into a semiloop before stalling and crashing.

Its forty-two-foot-ten-inch wingspan made the Hellcat somewhat larger than many of the first-line fighters of its day, including the Zero. The wings were squared-off in the typical Grumman fashion that had been

Underside of early F6F-3 shows how the main gear neatly swiveled 90 degrees and then folded back into the trailing-edge portion of the wing. (National Air & Space Museum)

started with the Wildcat. The tip chord was sixty-five inches and the leading and trailing edge tapered inward to the root chord, which measured 123 inches. The planform produced an overall wing area of 334 square feet, enough to make the Hellcat capable of turning on a dime—just the ticket when taking on the Zero. The tip airfoil was a NACA 23009 that tapered into the heavier-section NACA 23015.6 (mod.) at the root.

The wing was divided into three sections: the center section and the two folding outboard sections. In general, the wing structure was built up of a multitude of formed ribs, two main spars and a wing flap/elevator spar. The framework was covered with flush-riveted formed sheet aluminum alloy. The wingtips were formed aluminum that were riveted to the outboard wing ribs. The various wing spars were built up of extruded aluminum cap strips with aluminum alloy webs. For strength the center section was covered with a heavier-gauge sheet than were the outer panels. Even that was reinforced with a doubler around the wheel wells.

The outer wings carried the machine guns, three fifty-caliber Brownings in each wing. The guns were normally provided with 200 rounds for each gun (about fifteen seconds worth); however, there were provisions that each gun could have 400 rounds for special combat operations. The guns were optically bore sighted to converge their fire at a 300-yard range. To mate with the gunsight above the instrument panel the guns were also mounted to fire slightly upward so that the point of fire conversion was in line with the gunsight.

A closeup of the F6F landing gear strut shows it to be of husky construction to withstand the rugged impact of carrier landings. The brake line and part of the retraction mechanism can also be seen. (National Air & Space Museum)

The guns were charged hydraulically with ammunition by turning the cockpit charging handle to the "charge" position and pushing in. The charging handle was located on the lower center control panel. The gun safety was engaged by turning the handle to the safety position and pushing in. The hydraulic hand pump was used to get the hydraulic system up to about 800 psi if the engine-driven system was not functioning. That way the guns could be charged or put in safety in such an emergency. The gun master switch and selector switches were located on the armament control panel on the pilot's right console.

Actual firing was done by depressing the trigger located on the forward side of the control stick. Electric heaters were clamped over the gun breeches to make sure the firing mechanism would work freely, since at altitudes where the temperatures were very cold, the gun's lubricants would be normally too stiff to allow firing. The pilot automatically benefited from the heaters, as they were wired directly to the aircraft's generator. There was a circuit breaker he might have to reset if the gun heating system dropped off the line due to some kind of transient spike in the electrical power.

It might be mentioned here that late in the Hellcat's career some models were fitted with two 20 mm cannon instead of the two inboard fifties in each wing. The cannon carried 250 rounds of shells. The ammunition boxes for all guns were accessible by removing panels on the top side of each wing. In the center-section leading edge near the left fuselage side was the gun camera.

The ailerons were fabric-covered, differential-controlled Frise types. The left one had a cockpit adjustable trim tab inset in its trailing edge while the right one had a ground-settable trim tab protruding from the trailing edge. The ailerons were double-cable operated by the control stick. The structure of the ailerons was similar to the elevators mentioned earlier.

The flaps were of all-metal construction and divided into four sections: two on the wing center section and one larger section on each outboard wing panel. The flaps were constructed of a multitude of ribs riveted to a formed sheet aluminum covering, resulting in a light sturdy structure. All four flaps operated in unison and were hydraulically actuated by a cylinder attached to each flap panel.

The F6F-3 shows off its somewhat brutish lines in this in-flight side view. Even though a large aircraft, its Pratt & Whitney R-2800 engine gave it a power-to-weight ratio that was more than equal to mixing it up with the smaller, lighter Japanese Zeros. (National Air & Space Museum)

The main landing gear had an eleven-foot tread. The gear rotated ninety degrees and folded backward into the wing in a trailing position. The rotation and backward movements took place simultaneously. Both gear legs were retracted by means of individual hydraulic cylinders. The gear legs were of heavy-duty, oleo-hydraulic shock-strut type. The gear rotated rearward about a steel pin on a heavy bronze bushing. Low-pressure balloon tires were mounted on cast magnesium wheels and fitted with hydraulic brakes.

The retractable tail wheel was fitted with a hard rubber tire and a hydraulic shock strut. A double-acting hydraulic cylinder retracted and extended it. The wheel could be locked straight ahead during landing and takeoff and could swivel 180 degrees for ground handling. A tricing tube hole was also located in the rear fuselage for ground handling.

Other Hellcat features included the pilot's ditching equipment. The materials consisted of a K-ration package, a seat pack and parachute, a life raft and paddle, a flotation jacket, water bottle, dye marker, a Gibson Girl radio and balloon with antenna, a first-aid kit, Very pistol and ammunition and, last of all, a fishing kit and knife. Of course he still had his service revolver.

The F6F-5 Hellcat was fitted with a target-tow hook and a target-release control located in the cockpit. That model aircraft was also equipped with a Type GR-1 automatic pilot. The auto-pilot could be engaged in a normal flight attitude and take over and continue in that attitude until changed with the automatic flight controller by the pilot.

While seldom needed in the South Pacific, windshield-deicing equipment was required for escort carrier duty in the North Atlantic by the Hellcat. The system consisted of a one-gallon anti-ice-fluid tank located forward of the firewall. The fluid was sprayed on the windshield as needed with a manual spray control valve. There was also a cockpit heating system consisting of a hot-air combustion-type heater that was electrically operated and controlled. The heater was not to be used during takeoff or landing or while in combat.

Also for cold-weather operation, there was an electrically energized engine-oil dilution system. The controls for the system were located on the fuel control panel and consisted of the oil-dilution control valve and the oil-diverter valve electric switch.

Late model Hellcats were fitted to accept six Mark V rocket launchers. They were mounted on pylons on the underside of each wing. The rockets were electrically fired singly, in pairs or in a ripple salvo. The sequence of firing was controlled by the pilot with a Mark III station distribution device installed in the cockpit.

The Hellcat was relatively docile to fly. It had to be, as many of its pilots were low time (just out of flight training) and quickly thrust into carrier warfare.

Getting ready for a flight in the Hellcat entailed first obtaining the aircraft's gross weight and loading condition. The pilot then entered the cockpit and began checking preflight requirements. His own comfort came first, so he adjusted the seat, rudder pedals, shoulder harness and rearview mirror. The landing gear control was checked to see that it was in the down position and the oxygen supply and regulator were checked for ready operation later. The mixture control should have been in idle-cutoff, the propeller at increase rpm, and the supercharger blower in neutral. Next items checked were the auxiliary fuel pump, the flap- and landing-gear-position indicators and the fuel tank quantities. Then came the gunsight illumination, armament controls and switches, radio controls and a quick note to see that the cowl flaps were open. If it was a night flight the gunsight illumination received particular attention, along with a test of all cockpit, recognition, formation, section, approach and landing lights. This all done and ok, the engine was ready to start.

A crewman outside the aircraft took over for a few minutes here to turn the prop through twelve or fifteen blades to make sure there was no residual gasoline or oil in the radial engine's lower cylinders. If the engine had been idle for an hour or more there was a good chance some oil had seeped past the rings and lay ready to bend a rod if the engine was power cranked. If such was the case, a spark plug was removed from each of the bottom cylinders so the oil could be ejected. With lower cylinders cleared it was time to crank up.

To start, the throttle was set about one-fifth open. That was to limit rpm until oil pressure started to build. Other prestart settings included mixture at idle-cutoff, supercharger at neutral, battery switch on

The British were the proud owners of this Hellcat F R Mk II, which was a photo-recon version of the F6F. This photo, taken in March 1945, shows the craft to be armed with eight rockets. (National Air & Space Museum)

and auxiliary fuel pump on. The primer switch was then held at "on" for three to five seconds and the ignition was switched to "on-both." With the starter switch "on" the engine should fire and the mixture control was advanced to auto-rich. The rpm level was kept below 1,000 until the oil temperature reached at least 40°C. If the oil pressure didn't get there within thirty seconds, the whole thing was shut down, as something was wrong.

Assuming the oil got up to temperature the engine was then warmed up with cowl flaps open, full low pitch prop, and 1,500 rpm. At this point a quick check of supercharger operation was run through, with a return of the supercharger control to neutral position when the check was finished. The next check was of the two magnetos at about 2,100 rpm and 30 in. Hg. manifold pressure. If the generator then showed full 28-volt output, the tail wheel was unlocked (on carriers) and the pilot was ready to roll.

The wings were spread and locked in place, if not already done. The engine was revved-up one last time to clear it, the cowl flaps were checked for half-open position, and the oil-cooler and intercooler shutters were set to full open. The mixture control was set to auto-rich, the supercharger control checked that it was still in neutral position and the prop put in full-increase-rpm position. The fuel selector was set for the right main tank and checked to make sure it was feeding at about 17 psi. The carburetor-protected air control should have been full-in and the manifold pressure at 54 in. Hg. The tail wheel was then checked to be in the locked position (unlocked for carrier operation), the cockpit canopy was full open, the cockpit heater off, the auxiliary fuel pump on and wing flaps down (if required). The rudder trim tab was set at two marks nose right to counteract engine torque. The aileron and elevator tabs were set at neutral.

Brakes off for takeoff acceleration and the wheels soon left the ground (or deck), and were ready to be immediately retracted—the sooner the better, as retraction allowed air speed to build more rapidly. The air speed was adjusted by throttle movement to reflect best climb speed, which was about 130 knots. The aircraft was trimmed as required and the instruments were again checked to make sure all was ok. If so, the auxiliary fuel pump could be shut down.

General flying characteristics of the Hellcat showed the craft to be stable at all normal loadings. Lowering the landing gear and the wing flaps did tend to make the plane a little nose-heavy. The Hellcat pilot, during a stall, found the right wing tending to drop slowly, along with a rather severe shaking of the aircraft. With power on and clean configuration, the nose dropped away at 62 knots—with power off, 64 knots. With everything down and dirty, but power on, the stall speed dropped to only 50 knots, 53 knots with the power off.

Spins. The pilots manual didn't say too much about them except what had been determined during controlled tests, by test pilots. Here is the verdict: "With the airplane loaded to 11,250 pounds, and the C.G. position at 26.00%, spins of four turns were investigated. A normal entry was made with ailerons one-half against the spin." In a right spin it was found the nose dropped to a fifty- to sixty-degree angle, that the aileron forces were negligible and the nose oscillation was the same frequency as the aircraft's rate of rotation. A recovery was made by applying full rudder reversal after 4½ turns, followed about one second later by full elevator reversal. The spin steepened sharply and the rate of rotation nearly doubled. With a loss of altitude of 5,000 feet, recovery and level flight was effected in about 1½ turns.

Left spins turned out to be not so bad. Recovery was effected in only 4,400 feet and with 1¾ turns. However, the nose oscillations were heavier and the aileron forces were greater, but the nose did not drop as steeply.

All in all, the aerobatic qualities of the aircraft were such that it could withstand about anything any pilot wanted to throw at it. However, due to the inability of the oil scavenger pump to operate inverted, upside-down flight was limited to about three seconds.

The pilots manual didn't discuss engine-out gliding, as there were too many variables to take into account. It was all pretty much up to the pilot to gain his own experience with the various weights the aircraft might be at when the glide occurred. The plane could be sideslipped with no problem.

Diving out of the sun to pounce on an unsuspecting enemy was the fighter pilot's dream come true. To accomplish it, however, there were a few things he had to remember from his aircraft manual. Limitations were that in a dive below 15,000 feet his IAS (indicated air speed) could not exceed 391 knots, the engine could not exceed 3,060 rpm. That was just part of it. He had to adjust his trim, make sure the canopy was closed and locked, the cowl flaps closed, the intercooler and oil cooler shutters closed and the supercharger control in neutral. The propeller control had

This trio of pictures shows F6F-5's from the Reserve Unit at NAS Floyd Bennett Field, New York. The international-orange Reserve fuselage strip is apparent as the background for the star and bar insignia. (Collect Air)

to be at 2,050 to 2,250 rpm. And the pilot could not allow manifold pressure to build up past thirty-four inches during the dive without retarding the throttle.

Other factors during a flight were more mundane but just as important; for instance, level flight. A batch of charts in the pilots manual helped him determine manifold pressures and throttle settings to achieve maximum range under various loading conditions—especially important when cruising over vast reaches of the ocean. The main rule for cruising was to maintain thirty-four inches of manifold pressure, or full throttle if above critical altitude. Maintaining 135 knots at the lowest feasible altitude did the most for range. The *best* was to fly at the lowest speed and altitude possible to achieve maximum range endurance.

The approach and landing could be made with or without power. The first step was to reduce air speed to about 120 knots. The second step was to open the canopy. This was particularly important during a carrier landing, in case the pilot found himself in the water. (With the canopy open it was much easier to depart the airplane in the water and head for the rescuers.) The fuel selector valve was set to the tank with the most fuel in it. The mixture control was then set to auto-rich with the propeller at about 2,350 rpm. As the altitude was low the supercharger was returned to the neutral position and the cowl flaps set at half-open position. If the landing destination was a carrier, the arresting hook was then extended, the oil cooler and intercooler flaps were set, the gear extended and the tail wheel unlocked. (For land operations it was locked.) About this time the wing flaps were lowered.

The landing characteristics of the Hellcat were excellent. At the conclusion of the landing run the wing flaps were immediately raised and (on the ground) the tailwheel was released. To keep from overheating the engine the cowl flaps were opened to the widest position. It was then a matter of taxiing back to the line and shutting down the engine.

HELLCAT HISTORY

CHAPTER VII

Grumman built two Hellcat prototypes. Robert L. Hall, test pilot of the Wildcat, was once more in the cockpit on June 26, 1942, when the first one lifted off for a successful test flight. The craft was powered by a Wright R-2600 engine and performed well. However, it didn't take long to make the decision to go for the new Pratt & Whitney R-2800 and really give the big fighter a kick in the pants. The 2,000 horsepower engine had been doing great on the inverted gull-wing F4U Corsair just across Long Island Sound at the Vought factory. The Navy was quick to agree. The engine change necessitated a rescrambling of the nomenclature alphabet, from XF6F-1 to XF6F-3. (The XF6F-2 was a later and separate turbocharger project that would never make the production grade.)

The Navy really went for the new Hellcat with the Pratt & Whitney engine and ordered it into production. It was an easy decision, for the Wildcat was not doing all that well against the nimble Zero. Also, the Corsair was showing signs of needing a lot of development work before it could be put into South Pacific carrier combat. But then there was a little setback.

Grumman needed a new factory in which to build the Hellcat but didn't really have any more priority in getting building materials than did many other defense equipment manufacturers who needed the same limited amount of brick, mortar and steel—particularly steel. In the late thirties the U.S. had shipped most of its scrap steel to Japan for making toys. Well, the general manager at Grumman, Leon A. Swirbul, wasn't going to give up easily. New York's Second Avenue El had been torn down, and the steel remains of the elevated railway were just lying there in a pile waiting for the junk dealer. The purchase of some of it provided Grumman with the structural steel needed to build Plant Three—home of the Hellcat.

The move was successful and Hellcats were coming down the production line even before the plant was finished. Unfortunately, the story got a little mixed up by the time it reached our people that were thousands of miles away in the South Pacific. The way they heard it was that the Hellcat itself was built from the Second Avenue El steel! It took a time for them to realize that was really not the case.

On October 3, 1942, Sheldon Converse, another Grumman test pilot, rode the first production Hellcat from the new factory into the air for a successful test flight. By the end of December, twelve of the new airframes had been put together and the wheels of Grumman production started to turn even faster, pushing Hellcats out the door at a rapidly increasing pace. To give an idea of the acceleration of production, a dozen

The first of the Hellcats was this XF6F-1 (BuAer 02981). This photo was taken in June 1942 at a time when the aircraft was still fitted with a Wright R-2600-16 Cyclone. The second prototype (XF6F-3, BuAer 02982) was fitted with the more powerful Pratt & Whitney R-2800 Twin Wasp, which provided more speed and climb ability. The number one aircraft shown was then changed over to the Pratt & Whitney engine. Both ships were then flown for flight-test evaluation of the new design. (Grumman)

more of the new fighters were out in January 1943; with thirty-five, eighty-one and 130 in February, March and April, respectively. Increased productivity continued to the point that by November the factory was turning out 400 Hellcats a month! The high production momentum was maintained and even grew to some degree, so that by March of 1945, 605 Hellcats were delivered to the Navy in one month!

Grumman engineers, while responsible for the simple straightforward design of the Hellcat that made it possible to be produced in such large numbers, could not take all the credit for the production success of the fighter. A great deal of it had to go to the 20,000 skilled, hard-working employees, who built the detail parts, then assembled them into finished Hellcats. That operation took about two-and-a-half-million square feet of under-roof space. The amazing thing was that before being employed by Grumman, the workers (many of them women) had never even been up close to an airplane, particularly one as sophisticated as the Hellcat. At any rate, shoe clerks, waitresses and other nontechnical workers provided the backbone for the massive effort to produce the fighter.

That effort was to stop the Japanese Zero fighter offense in the South Pacific. They were a non-union work force and they were a happy lot. Grumman had only about half the quit-rate of other wartime industries. The reason? There was an all-out effort on the part of Grumman management to make the workers loyal and contented with the company's direction. The company nurtured a family atmosphere with dances, air

The XF6F-2 (BuAer 66244) was nicknamed *Fuzzy Wuzzy* because of the tufts attached to its skin to study airflow over the plane. The aircraft featured the Birmann turbo-supercharger, which, due to repeated danger from engine exhaust fires, was soon abandoned. (Grumman)

shows, day care centers, sports and every other fringe benefit it could think of, to keep the rank and file happy and it was successful in almost every respect.

This atmosphere also pervaded the in-plant work life and workers were instilled with a sense of pride and accomplishment that made them put forth their best productive efforts. Later in the war the Navy got more Hellcats out of the Bethpage facility than it knew what to do with. So Grumman cut its employment rolls by about five percent to slow the flow of fighters, to match the Navy's requirements. It didn't work. The workers on the job *increased* production for the next month by about twenty aircraft. Management then decided to get rid of another five percent of the production employees. That didn't work either. Still more planes that were not scheduled were produced. No more workers were laid off. The Navy couldn't have stood the increased production!

Since the Grumman plant was such a folksy and homey place to work it was not surprising that the management people were a type that, while extremely competent, were given to somewhat liberal views and actions. That was true of the boss himself, LeRoy Grumman. He decided, one day in 1944, that he ought to fly a Hellcat, even though he had not flown *anything* in a number of years.

Over everyone's protests, including those of test pilot Converse, who gave Grumman a ten-minute cockpit check, the "old man" was determined. Years before when he had had business problems he would go for a mind- and worry-easing flight and return refreshed and ready for business again. Now he wanted to do the same thing. This time, though, it was in a machine that was a quantum jump beyond anything he had ever flown before. It was a tribute to the design and performance of the Hellcat

The three-color finish used during late 1943 shows up well on this F6F-3. (Collect Air)

Toward war's end some Hellcats were converted to radio-controlled target drones. Such was the case of this F6F-5K that was converted from an F6F-5 fighter. (National Air & Space Museum)

that he got away with it. He took off and soon flew out of the field's traffic pattern. Returning later he made a greased-on landing before taxiing back to the flight line.

All was well until he disembarked and found himself confronted by the outstretched palms of several test pilots. He had forgotten to raise the flaps during the taxi back to the line. That error cost a dollar. The buck was to go into the party-kitty. Grumman handed over a fiver after he complained some about his lack of experience in a Hellcat. He wasn't being a big spender, however. He confided to the assembled test pilots that he *might* have done some other illegal things they hadn't seen during his twenty-minute sojourn in the Hellcat! That type of thinking was what made the whole Grumman organization tick from top to bottom. It created the esprit de corps that made it such a great aircraft manufacturer even when the going got rough.

Then Charles Lindbergh had a crack at the Hellcat. He was affiliated in a rather loose way with the Corsair factory across Long Island Sound. As a result of close proximity, and the close relationship among test pilots, there was bound to be occasional unofficial swapping of test aircraft between the test pilots of Grumman and Chance Vought. They were both building hot fighters for the Navy and both the fighters were

The F6F-6 shown here was one of two built to explore the use of four-blade Hamilton Standard propellers. While no production was undertaken, the craft was the fastest of the Hellcats with a top speed of 417 miles per hour at 22,000 feet. (Grumman)

powered by the same big Pratt & Whitney R-2800. It was all good clean fun and the parent companies didn't mind, as it gave their test pilots a broad experience when they got down to business evaluating the company product.

Lindbergh had trundled over to the Grumman field in a borrowed Corsair and had already been recognized in the men's room. It seems that when one is famous there is no place to hide! Once out of the men's room he quietly let it be known that he would like to try on the wings of a Hellcat. (No matter what that hero did, it was always with the soft pedal pushed full-down.) A Grumman test pilot readily agreed to let him have a go at the plane, a new F6F. After a complete cockpit checkout for the walking-on-water Lindy, he was let go to his own devices in the just-off-the-line Hellcat.

The engine started up without a problem. The takeoff was without a problem. The flight of about a half hour was without a problem. Then the problem: The landing gear would not come down. The thought of Lindy being wiped out in a gear-up landing of a Hellcat was more than anyone could bear to even contemplate. Mechanics and engineers, and anyone else with a good idea, headed for the control tower to spew out advice enough to fill a couple volumes of *Britannica*. He followed some of it and after a few dives with abrupt pullouts the stubborn gear came down and even locked.

Thus two pilots, one a great hero in the conquest of the air over the Atlantic, and the other a fifty-year-old executive and founder of one of the world's great aeronautical manufacturing companies, flew the Hellcat. It was a first flight in the aircraft for both. Both completed their flight safely even though the aircraft was on the leading edge of aviation technology. While a tribute to the pilots' skills, it was also a tribute to the forgivingness and docility built into the aircraft. It was once said that the Hellcat

A postwar F6F-5N shows off its radar pod located under the right wing. These craft were often used as night fighters during the Pacific war. (Collect Air)

was a plane built by shoe clerks to be flown by shoe clerks in a manner that would challenge the most professional military pilots of the world, the Japanese. And it did! The Grumman Hellcat was one more example of the company's ability to produce an exciting, first-line fighter plane. It could take on with parity and success any fighter aircraft it might have to defend itself against.

Compared with the Wildcat, there were few distinct models of the Hellcat. Basically, the Wildcat started as a biplane, progressed through several models of experimental ships with short rounded-tip wings and tails and eventually wound up not looking at all like the original aircraft. The Hellcat, after a model that used the Wright 2600 engine, as mentioned, went right on to use the Pratt & Whitney R-2800 and started flying off the new Grumman production lines, headed for combat, as a full-fledged, developed fighter.

The prototype XF6F-1 was completed and in the air on June 26, 1942, just a little short of a full year after the June 30, 1941, contract date for a new fighter between Grumman and the Navy. The idea had been to design a new fighter that was powerful, well armed and able to take on the Zero.

The plane was rugged enough in construction that it could take it as well as dish it out. A lot of pilots came home in it after their plane was riddled with gunfire to the point few other aircraft would have been able to return. As for dishing it out, the Hellcat was a very big and stable gun platform oozing with the firepower belted out by the six fifties. Bob Hall's first flights, even with the Wright engine, showed the aircraft superior to the Wildcat. Then the Pratt & Whitney R-2800 became available. It put out 2,000 horsepower and the jump in size provided the Hellcat with a twenty-five percent higher performance level.

The XF6F-3 was similar in design to the prototype XF6F-1 but it started out with the R-2800 Pratt & Whitney. It was in the air on July 22, 1942, piloted by the capable, experienced hands of test pilot Hall. The *first* prototype, after an engine change to the new Pratt & Whitney, also became an XF6F-3. The two XF6F-3's were used for all the test work required to get the Hellcat into production.

A few items made them different from any subsequent Hellcats: the large propeller spinners initially fitted and the unpainted natural aluminum airframe, neither of which lasted past the prototypes. Another readily recognizable item was the large, main landing-gear wheel well covers. For real nitpickers, the two XF6F-3's could be distinguished from each other by the pitot tube locations and the size of the exhaust port

This Hellcat tries out Tiny Tim rocket firing at China Lake NAV ORD TEST STA. Rockets were used against ground targets and were not intended for air-to-air operations. (National Archives)

openings near the leading edges of the wings. The pitot was perched above the right wingtip of the first aircraft (02981) and slung below the right wingtip on the second model (02982). Another small change was that the side engine exhaust pipe port openings were smaller on the second ship than on the first. There were, of course, other minor internal details that were changed based on things learned building the first prototype.

In October the first *production* Hellcat appeared—talk about moving right along! Although these first production F6F-3 planes still retained the large landing gear wheel covers, it wasn't long before they became smaller and more streamlined. A Hamilton Standard Hydromatic propeller replaced the Curtiss Electric and the massive propeller spinner was dropped. As usual, the reason for the last deletion was to allow the engine to be cooled more effectively. While a spinner looked good, and certainly added to the streamlining of a radial engine, its results always seemed to come out the same. With that big cone in front of an air-cooled radial there never seemed to be enough air to cool the cylinders. Many aircraft designers have tried it and hardly any have been successful. Those that have, usually settled for a somewhat smaller spinner than that used on the

A not-the-best-of-snapshots of a Hellcat somewhere on a Pacific island during the latter days of World War II. However, it shows the scene as it was. (Collect Air)

Hellcat prototypes. The cowling on the production machine was redesigned a little in the area of the exhaust ports.

On January 16, 1943, the Navy accepted its first production Hellcat. By the end of that year over 2,500 of them had been delivered and they were in heavy use in the Pacific, knocking down Zeros.

During the war years production problems came up that were fixed on demand. More range was needed at times so the centerline drop tank was instituted. The early production F6F-3 had the 2800-10 engine but a -10W water-injection engine was soon substituted, giving the Hellcats a still greater advantage over the Zero when a sudden burst of speed was needed. Great Britain received a share of the 4,402 F6F-3's completed by April 1944—252 in all.

The paint jobs on the Navy's F6F-3's were generally sea blue on the top surfaces, intermediate blue (blue-gray) on the sides and flat white on the undersurfaces. The national insignia on the wings and fuselage sides run the gamut from the white star in a dark blue circle, the white star on a blue circle with white bars, the whole star design surrounded in red and, of course, the white star and bars as was used after the war.

Another feature of the earlier models of the F6F-3 was the streamlined covers on the leading edge of the wings for the machine gun barrels. Early F6F-3's had different windshield assemblies than later models. They were fitted with a horizontal cross-piece above the windshield (later eliminated). The cowl flaps located on either side of the lower cowl were also eliminated as production proceeded. All these little things were changed on an ongoing basis to make the F6F-3 ever easier to produce due to simplification. Add up enough of those little changes and several more planes could be produced each week with the same amount of manpower. Today the concept has been rediscovered and it's called Value-Analysis, the latest and greatest technique in the engineering world!

There were two sub-species of the F6F-3 Hellcats, somewhat different than the general breed of cat. They were the radar-equipped night-fighter versions: the F6F-3N and the -3E models. They could be easily spotted, for each had a cylindrical housing on the right wing near the tip that enclosed the all-seeing radar dish. They entered carrier combat in late November 1943, and soon proved to be valuable new additions to the carrier's capabilities. They could seek out a nighttime enemy without ever actually seeing him and then destroy him while still in the darkness. However, the attack was usually in enough light (moonlight, exhaust flames, formation lights, etc.) to be pressed home with the enemy aircraft fully visible to the naked eye.

A loose training formation of F6F-3's late in 1943. (Collect Air)

The exterior difference between the N and E models was the position of the radome. The -3E carried the pod for its AN/APS-4 radar slung under the wing while the -3N model housed its AN/APR-6 radar streamlined and faired smoothly into the wing. The radar screen was located high on the instrument panel where the pilot could read the range and position of the enemy by means of a blip located on a cathode ray tube, then home-in for an attack. The actual electronics equipment was mostly located in the fuselage bay behind the pilot. About 200 F6F-3N's were built versus only eighteen of the -3E models. The latter were really only for tryout of the scheme and when found successful, were supplanted by the more-finished-off -3N's.

Before continuing with the Hellcat's evolution it would be well to go back and pick up the XF6F-2 and XF6F-4 models of which only one of each was built.

The XF6F-2 was started at the same time as the -1 and -3 models to try out the idea of using a turbo-supercharger on the Pratt & Whitney R-2800. As it turned out, the first flight was not until January 7, 1944. The major drawback with the aircraft (66244) was danger of fire due to the Birman supercharger pumping raw gasoline into the engine's exhaust. The desired end result of the program was to increase the engine's performance at 20,000 feet to equal what it could do at sea level. The earlier Wright engine, supercharged the same way, also had been considered for this aircraft, but that project died.

The XF6F-4 was a rehash of the first prototype (02981) to show the possibility of mounting four 20 mm aircraft cannon in the wings with 200 rounds per gun. The aircraft was tested at the Patuxent River Naval Air Station Test Facility in October 1942. In a few short months the prototype had gone from a Wright-powered fighter, to a Pratt & Whitney-powered fighter, and to the four-cannon model. The same plane, in that short time, had been an XF6F-1, XF6F-3 and then XF6F-4. Grumman finally refurbished the plane as an F6F-3 and sent it off to the war as a fighter, a somewhat unusual thing in itself as prototype aircraft seldom wind up pulling actual service duty. One other change on that particular aircraft as finalized was the engine—updated to a Pratt & Whitney R2800-27.

The next Hellcat was the F6F-5, the improved version of an already proven and satisfactory design. It was built in the largest numbers, 7,870 units (after production of the -3 stopped). The -5 had a strengthened airframe and a smaller, more close-fitting engine cowl. Other features included the ability to carry underwing ordnance, such as six five-inch HVAR rockets or two 1,000-pound bombs under the fuselage. A flat-

With full flaps this F6F-5 prepares to make a graceful three-point touchdown. (Collect Air)

As Grumman's learning curve developed, the Hellcat was produced in ever increasing numbers to the point the Navy finally had to ask for a reduction in manufacturing even though the war was still going on! (Collect Air)

fronted windshield was also fitted to give the pilot better undistorted vision when using the reflector gunsight, especially at night. The bomb racks could also be used to carry drop tanks, mainly for long ferry flights. Some -5's were fitted with two 20 mm cannon, one in each wing, in addition to two fifty-caliber machine guns in each wing. The cannon never really caught on very well with the Navy pilots, and many aircraft so equipped were later changed back to the standard six fifty-caliber configuration.

The performance was improved a bit and the -5 could climb to 20,000 feet in about seven minutes. And it could scoot along at 380 miles per hour at 23,000 feet. There was nothing shabby about that performance when compared to any other production fighter around at the time. Of course, the little picture cards that came on the back of Wings cigarette packs during the war had every Allied fighter rated at over 400 miles per hour including the Hellcat, but that was seldom true, particularly when a plane was loaded with full armament and full fuel tanks.

It was the last of the Hellcat production runs and except for a few running changes, such as removing the fuselage side windows located aft of the canopy, the F6F-5B was a pretty stable design. England got 9,300 of them for use on its escort carriers. As the war drifted to a close, France and Uruguay picked up a few for their naval air arms. A total of 12,274 Hellcats were produced.

There were, of course, several sub-models of the -5. These included the -5E and -5N radar models for night fighting and the -5K and -5P models. The -5K's were radio-controlled target drones and the -5P's were

There were a lot of Hellcats around after World War II and they continued in service up through the late forties when the first operational carrier jets began to take over. This mini-album shows what they looked like at service at various bases. One was even slicked up and used for static display so that wartime taxpayers could view close-up the type of aircraft that all that money went for. (Collect Air)

photo recon aircraft with aerial cameras mounted in the aft fuselage. Paint jobs on these aircraft were generally all sea blue instead of the three-color motif used on the earlier F6F-3's. The drone missions used more colorful paint jobs, like bright orange with white stripes on the fin and wings. The most exciting thing the drones did was fly into the atomic mushroom clouds during the A-bomb tests at Bikini Atoll.

The final version of the Hellcat was the F6F-6, of which two were built. Their claim to fame was the use of Hamilton Standard four-blade propellers and the 2,100 horsepower Pratt & Whitney R2800-18W engines. First flown on July 6, 1944 (the second craft on August 30, 1944), by test pilot P. Gallo, the planes showed themselves able to really move out—417 miles per hour! The airframe numbers were 70188 and 70913 and they would have been the prototype of the next big production run of Hellcats if the war had not ended.

HELLCAT WARRIORS

CHAPTER VIII

August 31, 1943, Marcus Island, West Pacific. The Hellcat was off on its first combat operation, a new aircraft but certainly not an unknown quantity. It was born of combat requirements of the early Pacific war, nurtured by reports from battle-scarred Wildcat pilots, created by the latest techniques of aerodynamic and manufacturing technology, and thoroughly tested to prove its ability. There was little doubt it would be a successful adversary for the Zero and anything else the Japanese might come up with in the foreseeable future.

Air Groups 9 and 5, flying off the carriers *Essex* and the new *Yorktown*, had carried out the attacks on Marcus Island. They didn't get to undertake any air-to-air combat but they did manage to strafe a few Betty bombers during the mission. It was an inauspicious but solid start. The next day Hellcats nailed their first aerial adversary. Lt. (JG) Richard L. Loesch and Ens. A. W. Nyquist shot down an Emily, a large 124-foot-span four-engined flying boat. The Hellcats seemed intent on Emilys, for they shot down another on the third of September, and still another on the eighth. Meanwhile a batch of the new Hellcats were flying CAP (combat air patrol) near their carriers. Since no one was attacking the carriers the CAP's were getting a lot of flight time but little action. They did manage to shoot down a stray Betty bomber during the next few weeks but that was it. More than a month would pass after the new Zero exterminator arrived on the scene before a real trial against an enemy fighter force would occur.

On October 5 and 6, 1943, VF-5, -6, -9, -16 and -22 made fighter strikes against Wake Island. VF-9 knocked down four enemy aircraft and its commanding officer, Edward "Butch" O'Hare of Wildcat fame, put away two of them, a Zero and a Betty. The Hellcat was blooded in battle.

Mentioning O'Hare also brings to mind the name David McCampbell. The Navy had only these two Congressional Medal of Honor pilots during the melee called World War II. They were the only airmen who had impressed peers and superiors with their heroism to the point that this high honor would be bestowed. As the war had worn on, the medal had become much harder to come by. Who was McCampbell? Well, for openers, he downed thirty-four Japanese aircraft during his wartime adventures. That accomplishment made him the Navy's highest ranking World War II ace.

Early in his career, obtaining that distinction did not look very promising—in fact, it was a downright dismal prospect. McCampbell was

An artful patriotic picture for the folks back home shows an F6F-3 running up aboard the USS *Nassau* (CVE-16), the American flag waving above its cowl. (National Archives)

from Bessemer, Alabama, when he entered Annapolis, gateway to a career as a Naval officer. He graduated in the class of 1933. That was great, except the whole class was discharged from the service, instead of being given a tour of active duty. Deep in the Depression the Navy had neither money nor berths for the new ensigns. It was back to Bessemer and a construction job for McCampbell.

By 1934 things were beginning to look up for the USN financially and McCampbell was called back to the Navy ranks. Aviation was a popular field for young officers and he attempted to get into pilot training. This was not unusual, for while out of the service, the Naval Academy graduate had tried to enter the Army Air Corps. The Army had said his eyesight was not good enough. Now the Navy said the same thing. A check by a civilian doctor said it was ok, however, so back he went to the Navy with a second application for flight training. This time he was accepted and by 1937 he was at Pensacola, Florida, a full-fledged flying candidate. Getting his gold wings led to duty aboard the USS *Ranger* with Fighting Squadron 4, flying first the F3F biplane and then the F4F monoplane Wildcat, over a two-year period.

The *Ranger* became attached to the Atlantic fleet in 1940, and in 1941 McCampbell transferred to the USS *Wasp*—still in the Atlantic—and half a world away from the South Pacific, where the action would soon be developing. It got even worse: Now he was no longer flying, for he was assigned the duties of an LSO (Landing Signals Officer). Not that it was a bad job; in fact, it was a very important one, but certainly not the way to become a combat ace.

F6F's on the flight deck of USS *Randolph* (CCV-15). (U.S. Navy)

Hellcats return from a strike on Formosa near the end of the war. One is accepted while the other is waved-off for a go-around and another try. (U.S. Navy)

In August 1942, the Navy finally sent the *Wasp* to the Pacific theater where the battle was churning around Guadalcanal. The *Wasp* supported the landings there but had the misfortune of being sunk by a Japanese submarine on September 15, 1942. McCampbell was a good swimmer and survived the disaster, although 324 crewmen did drown. After he was rescued he was sent home for some well-earned R and R. Following the rest and relaxation it was back to duty as an LSO instructor.

In the summer of 1943 the United States was definitely on the offensive. The Navy needed exprienced pilots to help out and McCamp-

While officers and enlisted men watch a movie in the background, ordnance people work on bombs on the hangar deck of the USS *Yorktown* (CV-10). Surrounding the scene are ever present F6F's. (U.S. Navy)

bell was given command of VF-15. He was totally inexperienced in combat, as were his men, but they bolstered up their egos with the unofficial name, The Fabled Fifteen. With most of the new squadron's pilots fresh from Pensacola, there were many hours of gunnery training and carrier operations to be put behind them before they were ready for a combat assignment. They were finally ready in the spring of 1944 and transferred to the carrier *Essex*.

On arrival, McCampbell was assigned command of the whole air contingent aboard the ship: fighters, dive bombers and torpedo bombers. One of his first missions was almost his last. His Hellcat's belly tank was hit, but he managed to drop it and continue on patrol. That was on May 14, 1944, over Marcus Island. He got back at the enemy on June 11, 1944, over Saipan when he bagged his first enemy aircraft. On June 14 the Japanese launched a massive counterattack consisting of nine carriers—a real armada of aerial clout. It was to be called the Battle of the Philippine Sea and the air was swarming with Japanese fighters. During two operational missions that day McCampbell bagged seven of them.

His score continued to grow and by September 1944 he had nineteen notches on his guns—almost a four-time ace. Running the whole

An F6F-3 flown by Wilbur B. "Spider" Webb of "Fighting Two" Squadron aboard the USS *Hornet* (CV-12) is having its wings folded for storage. It was June 1944 and it had just been in a raid over the Marianas. (U.S. Navy)

aircraft show on the *Essex* required a bit of desk work as well as piloting a Hellcat. McCampbell was doing his paperwork in the VF-15 ready room on October 24, 1944. There were only seven pilots left aboard the *Essex* that day. Everyone else had been launched on a big mission against the island of Luzon. It was a quiet day aboard the carrier until, "All pilots report to their aircraft!" The *Essex* radar had picked up about sixty enemy aircraft, bombers and fighters heading their way.

McCampbell and his wingman, Roy Rushing, pounded into the air to intercept about forty Japanese fighters flying cover for twenty bombers intent on blowing the *Essex* out of the water. McCampbell quickly dispatched the five other Hellcats to knock down as many bombers as they could before they reached the *Essex*. He and his wingman would try to keep the enemy fighters busy. The enemy fighters, however, were low on fuel and the last thing they wanted was a dogfight—even with only two Hellcats.

VF-9 F6F-5's get ready for a catapult takeoff aboard the USS *Lexington* on February 25, 1945. (U.S. Navy)

McCampbell and Rushing jumped the formation from above, picking off several, then zoomed for altitude to repeat the maneuver. The Japanese fighters finally broke their formation and began flying in a counterclockwise defensive circle. That forced the two Hellcat pilots into making head-on attacks. They did so but took several hits themselves in the process. The enemy fighters finally broke up and headed for home, McCampbell and Rushing in hot pursuit. McCampbell accounted for nine kills that day. With them, the Medal of Honor was on its way.

Being low on fuel, getting back to the *Essex* was now out of the question so why not land on the nearby *Hornet?* The *Hornet* wasn't having any of it. Strange planes were shot at by the gun-shy crews. The *Langley* finally did let him aboard. That evening after everything had calmed down, and his plane refueled, McCampbell flew it back to the *Essex* to sleep in his own bunk.

In early November 1943, America was on the march against the concentration of naval and air strength the Japanese had built up at Rabaul. The Hellcats were to fly cover for TBF Avengers and SBD Dauntlesses, torpedo and dive bombers. The Japanese retaliated to defend their bastion; and soon the Hellcats were in the middle of a swarming aerial firefight. Over the island's Simpson Harbor, fighting was thickest and when it was over twenty-two enemy aircraft had been shot down, plus seventeen listed as probable hits. Hellcat losses numbered three. (It's a fact that light losses are generally glossed over in combat reports. That's great—unless you were a part of the light losses.)

The F6F's were back at Rabaul the next day flying through heavy pea-soup weather. They were once more escorting the more ponderous dive and torpedo bombers when a swarm of Japanese protectors rose to meet them. This time the score for the USN was thirty-one enemy aircraft destroyed with an additional five probables. (One of the kills was a bit bizarre when William Blair of VF-9 accidentally picked off a Zero by

A fully loaded F6F Hellcat takes off in front of a waiting SBD. The small deck of a "Jeep" carrier is readily apparent in this photo. (U.S. Navy)

dropping his belly tank on it. It was unusual, but effective. Blair couldn't have repeated the maneuver for a million dollars!)

Back at the carriers, things were beginning to get a little hot. The *Independence, Bunker Hill* and *Essex* were within range of the Japanese. . . . As a second American strike on Rabaul was about to begin, a flock of irate Val dive bombers and some older Kates suddenly appeared. As the Hellcats had barely gotten off the flight deck it was a bit unnerving for the Navy pilots. "Billy" Watts, last F6F off the *Bunker Hill* almost didn't get his wheels up before he had a successful shot at a Val. After about an hour the enemy retreated; the carrier task force had managed to get away unscathed. VF-9 claimed forty-one kills, VF-18 claimed 20½, and VF-22 claimed one. While those figures were undoubtedly inflated by the swirling heat of combat, they did represent a tremendous aerial victory for the still new Hellcat in plane-to-plane combat. The Grumman was

F6F-5's of VF-12 aboard the USS *Randolph* (CCV-15) during May to July of 1945. (National Archives)

definitely a winner and was doing everything its designers had said it would do.

In November and December of 1943 operation GALVANIC, to conquer the Gilbert Islands, took place. Six CV's (large carriers), five CVL's (light carriers) and eight CVE's (light escort carriers) embarked on the mission. By now the F6F's had become plentiful enough that only three of the CVE's did not have Hellcats aboard. Rather than meet the attack task force head-on the Japanese conducted mainly torpedo bomber attacks during the night. The cover of darkness gave their low-flying bombers a certain amount of protection. The thought of a carrier-based night fighter became very attractive. Wildcat Medal of Honor winner Butch O'Hare decided to give night operations a try, being led to the enemy by a radar-equipped TBF Avenger. The Avenger managed to shoot down two Bettys but O'Hare was lost on the mission, presumably shot down during his search in the dark for the enemy.

The Hellcats continued to get the better of the Zeros as the Navy began to push the Japanese back across the South Pacific. On December 4, twelve VF-16 Hellcats ripped into an enemy formation over Kwajalein. Out of thirty Zero targets available, nineteen were shot down—and a Betty for good measure! Next was the melee over the Marshall Islands in early

USS *Nassau* (CVE-16) accepts one F6F-3 while the following one is waved-off so that the flight deck can be cleared for the next landing. (National Archives)

1944. New carriers were added to the fleet and along with them large quantities of Hellcats fresh from the Grumman assembly lines.

The Japanese fortress of Truk was next, thought by many to be impregnable. The problem was that nobody told the Hellcat pilots. Seventy-two of the husky Grummans arrived over the atoll at dawn on February 16, 1944. About fifty Japanese fighters were in the air already and more were taking off. In what was probably the fiercest dogfight in the Pacific air war, the Hellcats lived up to their name. With a loss of only four of their own, fifty Japanese fighters were knocked down. That was more than an eight-to-one kill ratio. Just to make their presence felt a little more, the Hellcats went on to strafe the remaining planes on the ground once they had wiped out the opposition in the air. The next day on their return to the target there was no airborne opposition to be found!

It was not all glory for the Navy, however, as the Japanese torpedo bombers kept making nighttime raids, and on several occasions damaged carriers with torpedo hits. As the fast carriers went farther westward into the Marianas a repeat of the Hellcat's Truk performance took place. This time the score was four F6F's lost to sixty-seven Japanese fighters lost—the Japanese had only 74 fighters in the air. Another hundred of the enemy machines were destroyed while still on the ground. With Grumman's high production back at Bethpage, and the Japanese losing aircraft

With lower cowl flaps open, this early F6F-3 comes in over the anchor chain of the USS *Nassau*. (National Archives)

right and left, the handwriting was on the wall: Japan was going to lose. . . .

The same sort of Hellcat success continued at Palau, Ulithi, Woleai, in the Western Carolines. Then came the Marianas. The Navy was well prepared with the largest carrier task force ever assembled—and the largest collection of Hellcats. Some 200 Hellcats took off on June 11, 1944, to roam the skies of Saipan, Tinian, Rota and Guam. During the day, more than seventy enemy planes were shot from the skies and more were destroyed on the ground. By June 13 there was no more Japanese air resistance in the Marianas.

However, on the nineteenth was the big carrier-versus-carrier battle and all hell broke loose. On that day the Hellcats claimed 354 kills—most from the enemy carriers that were trying to make a last-ditch air counterattack against the marauding Hellcats. Only eighteen F6F's were lost and one of those only because of an operational accident! With that low loss ratio it was no wonder the Navy was pleading with Grumman to slow up production of the Hellcats.

During the campaign for Iwo Jima the night-fighting radar-equipped F6F-3N's and -5N's became operational. This was something new, for instead of being vectored toward a target by a mother-hen TBF, the new Grumman night fighters carried self-contained radar mounted on their outboard right wings. Though untried in combat, the theory seemed good. The task force commanders were at first a little hesitant to use the planes in such a manner but soon the objections were overcome and the night-flying Grummans were patrolling the dark skies over the fleet.

In addition to the night fighers, there was the F6F-5P photo-recon version. Even the pilots of some of these planes became aces. But they were admonished to "Quit shooting down planes and get on with your photo job!" It did not seem fair to be crucified for becoming an ace but, then, war *is* hell.

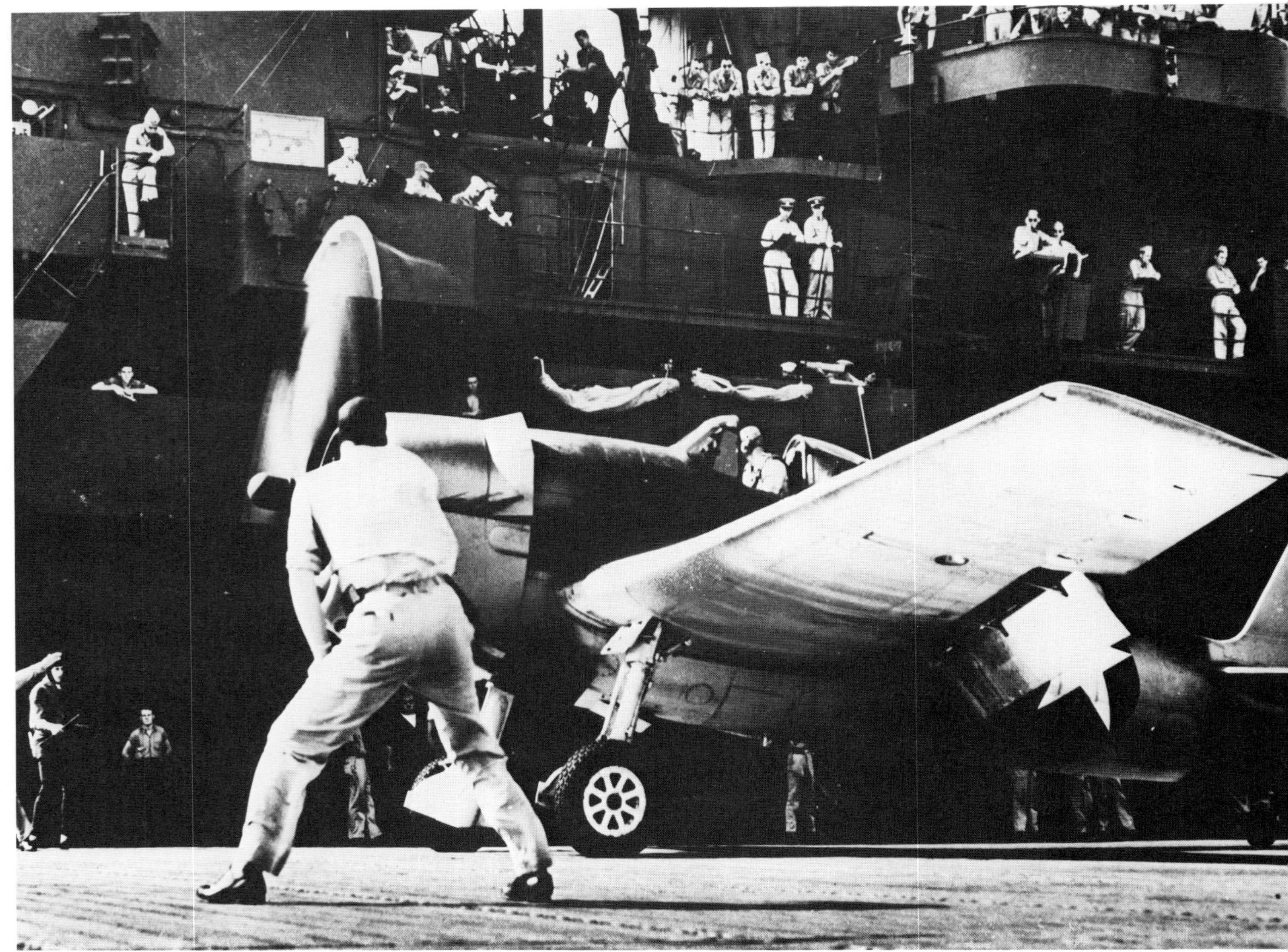

F6F-3 taking off past the bridge of the USS *Badger.* (National Archives)

By October 12, 1944, the Hellcats were really getting close to the Japanese home territory, Formosa. The closer they got the more planes the enemy put up in defense. However, although the Japanese had fighter planes in significant numbers, their supply of experienced pilots was just about exhausted. Their new pilots were green to the strategy of aerial combat and made fairly easy targets for the U.S. Navy and Marine pilots who were now getting to be old hands at the job. The F6F pilots over Formosa, even though outnumbered by as much as five to one, knocked down over 300 enemy aircraft with a loss of only twenty-seven Hellcats.

The Philippines (Luzon, Clark Field, Manila) also received attention from the Hellcats. The Japanese had lost their taste for aerial combat because of their horrendous losses. Since the enemy fighters would not come up to meet them, the F6F's simply started strafing the enemy aircraft on the ground. It was a lot less hazardous to the pilots on both sides and, with the enemy's inexperienced airmen considered, the results were about the same. As the battle for the Philippines continued the night-fighter Grummans came even more into play and successfully shot down

F6F Hellcats and F4U Corsairs line up on a coral strip at Espiritu Santo in February 1944. The fighter units are unknown. Note that F6F-3 Battling Bobbie, in foreground, has its radio mast replaced by a whip antenna. (National Archives)

many night intruders, some without ever seeing their quarry until it burst into flames when hit.

About this time kamikaze tactics were being used by the Japanese. More and more the "one-way-ticket" Japanese attacks resulted in severe damage to, and in some cases sinking of, U.S. ships. The carrier pilots were kept hard at it trying to destroy these piloted, guided missiles before they could reach the surface fleet. In many cases the pilots had a high stake in the outcome of their efforts, for the enemy's target could very well be the pilot's carrier.

Okinawa. The battle for that island stronghold was without doubt one of the most important in drawing the noose tighter around the enemy mainland. The only way the Japanese could even hope to stop its invasion was through the use of kamikaze aircraft. The best protection against the kamikazes was to shoot them down before they ever reached the area of the fleet. That job fell to the Hellcat pilots. There were, of course, the usual Oscars and Zekes packed with explosives, but a new menace was soon seen in numbers: the Oka. The Oka was a small, piloted glide bomb that was carried to the target area by a Betty bomber. Once released at altitude

F6F-5N's of VF(N)-107 from Quonset Point, Rhode Island. Aircraft were finished in glossy sea blue when photographed in August 1945. Radomes housed AN/APS-6 radar. (National Archives)

the little glider went like hell toward the fleet, its nose cone loaded with TNT and its pilot loaded with religious fervor to die honorably for the homeland.

The best way to beat this tactic was to shoot down the Betty with its Oka before the pair got within range of the ships. To make this tougher the Japanese generally sent a batch of Zekes along with the Betty formations to cover them. As an example, on March 21, 1945, eighteen Bettys protected by thirty Zekes attempted an attack on the fleet. Sixteen of the Bettys carried Oka suicide glide bombs. The attack was met by sixteen Hellcats. Again the final score was lopsided in favor of the Americans. All eighteen Bettys and twelve of the Zekes were destroyed with the loss of only one F6F. Over the period the Japanese lost over 800 aircraft to the Hellcat's Browning fifties. During this same period about eight F6F's were downed, generally from anti-aircraft fire, which could not be avoided, no matter how great the pilot's skill and determination.

During the Okinawa campaign the Hellcat also saw some foreign service. On March 26 British carriers had joined the U.S. Navy off the coast of Okinawa and some of its fighter units received Hellcats from the Lend-Lease program.

The Grumann Hellcat Mk. II is shown here in British Royal Navy markings. (National Air & Space Museum)

With Okinawa now a secured forward base for the American B-29's the real attack on mainland Japan got under way. The fast carriers, both British and American, began cruising along the coast of the mainland in July and August. The Hellcats were used to strafe fighter-bombers over Japan, with little resistance shown by the Japanese Air Force. What planes the enemy did have left were kept concealed for use at a later date when the invasion of their home islands came. That was expected to occur in October. Of course October never came for the Japanese war effort. On August 6 the first atomic bomb was dropped on Hiroshima and, on August 9, a second on Nagasaki. It was only a matter of days until the shooting came to a halt. So did Hellcat production—finally.

Of the 1,182 Hellcats delivered to Britain under Lend-Lease many saw combat in the European theater of operations, such as carrier-launched antishipping strikes along the Norwegian coast. When the German battleship *Tirpitz* was attacked in Kaafiord, Hellcats made up a part of the fighter contingent. Most of the fighter's use, however, was with the Far East operations of the British Navy. Many Asian areas such as the Malayan coast, Rangoon, Isthmus of Kra, Penang and Northern Sumatra became the stomping grounds for the British Hellcats. One batch even ended up in South Africa. After the war, with the exception of a few museum pieces, the F6F's were returned to the United States, in keeping with the Lend-Lease agreement.

After the war the Hellcat was somewhat out of business. For one thing, the new F8F Grumman Bearcat could run rings around it in all departments including speed, agility and climb. For another, the new jets that were coming along would make any piston-engine fighter archaic, even the spiffy Bearcat. However, some Naval Air Reserve units received the type until the early fifties. The Hellcat also served as an advanced trainer for the new generation of naval pilots before they transitioned to the first jets. A few Hellcats remained in first-line service until the mid-fifties but they were special-purpose aircraft such as the F6F-5N radar-

Cowl flaps open, wing flaps down, belly tank full, engine at takeoff rpm, this F6F launches against the backdrop of the carrier island. (Collect Air)

equipped night fighters. Some others were configured as drones and flown though the atomic hell clouds of the Bikini A-bomb tests in 1946.

They had one last shot at combat in August 1952, during the Korean War. Six of the pilotless drone Hellcats were converted to guided-missile configuration and launched from the Boxer CV carrier against a railroad bridge at Hungnam. After takeoff they were controlled on the way to the target by AD Skyraiders. A few Hellcats are now restored and in flying condition. A few more are on display at various air museums around the world. Small numbers were transferred or sold to the French for use in Indochina and several more were taken over by the Uruguayan Naval Air Arm.

While it is true the F6F didn't last long after the war, it was in good company: neither did the Republic P-47 nor the Martin B-26, both also classed as first-line aircraft in the war against the Axis. The only reason the Hellcat was ever designed and built was to have a naval carrier fighter superior to the Zero. That it was, but when the Zero was gone there just wasn't any more need for the Hellcat.

CHAPTER IX NINE-LIVED CATS

The first of the famous fighters by Grumman were the F2F and F3F series of flying barrel biplanes harking back to the early and mid-thirties. Those were the days when seagoing aviation was becoming an important consideration for U.S. defense. The retract-geared machines were doubtless the most exotically colorful warbirds to be found during that period. Public interest in the aircraft was enhanced by their appearance, along with such stars as John Wayne and Robert Taylor, in several movies during the late thirties.

The new design of the F4F series by Grumman was still a biplane, but on paper only. The proposed fighter was soon nudged along into a more modern configuration, the monoplane F4F-2 that was to become the Wildcat. The change was a reaction to the introduction of the competitive Brewster Buffalo.

The next Grumman effort, the F5F, was a real design departure for the firm, a twin-engine fighter. It was ordered by the Navy on June 30, 1938, and it was to be the last word in flying gun platforms, carrying four 23 mm Masden cannon and forty anti-aircraft bombs in the wings. That last item was a bit unusual to say the least.

Named the Skyrocket, the first XF5F-1 flew on April 1, 1940. It really caused a buzz in the aviation press. It certainly *looked* different than anything anyone had seen before (or since, for that matter). Two big, nine-cylinder Wright R-1820-40 Cyclone engines belted out 1,200 horsepower each at 2500 rpm. They were mounted close-in to the center of the forty-two-foot-span, squared-off wing. The fuselage nose never quite got to the wing's leading edge. Instead it took on kind of a hanging-on-for-dear-life appearance as it lay atop the wing with several inches of leading edge extending ahead of it. Except for the engine nacelles the wing's leading edge was unbroken from tip to tip—on a low-wing fighter plane! The overall length of the bizarre Grumman creation was twenty-eight feet 8.5 inches.

The leading gear retracted into the massive engine nacelles, with the tail wheel sporting a streamlined enclosure that hung beneath the fuselage. The twin tails of the craft were squared off (a Grumman trademark) and set at the end of a distinctly dihedral elevator and stabilizer. The fuselage was little more than a straight-back monocoque box structure that really had no shape but did hold the tail to the wings and engines to make a complete aircraft. On top of the fuselage sat a large greenhouse for the pilot enclosure, which gave excellent visibility in all directions. It if were not for the pane frames it would have been very much like a modern bubble canopy.

The whole squared-off design (one sometimes wonders if a French curve ever existed in the Grumman drafting room) was light for its size and horsepower. It weighed in at 9,478 pounds. That, plus the sizzling power, gave the F5F an initial rate of climb of 4,000 feet per minute. It was somewhat greater than the contemporary F3F's 2,650 feet per minute. With all that horsepower and so little airplane, top speed was right up there too: 380 miles per hour at 16,500 feet. And the whole project only cost $112,000.

Noted in the Grumman project accounting system as design G-34 (the production Wildcats were G-36's), the prototype was around for quite a while as the Navy tried to figure it out. Flown by B. A. "Bud" Gillies for the first time, and many flights thereafter, the prototype was evaluated by Grumman from April 1, 1940, till February 22, 1941—in all, over seventy test flights were made. The prototype then was sent off to NAS Anacostia for the Navy to wrestle with it. It did, for a while, then sent the ship back to Grumman on April 28 for a hydraulic system overhaul and improved engine nacelles.

Even though the originally planned heavy armament was never installed, two fifties and two thirties were finally mounted in the nose. Improved cowls were to help out with engine cooling; always, it seemed, a bear of a problem with a new aircraft.

Original schemes were always reconsidered for improvement, hence the variety of dash numbers for an aircraft. Before the ship was returned to NAS Anacostia July 24, 1941, several apparent changes had been made during the aerodynamic cleanup of the Skyrocket. All of them made sense, but in a way it was a shame, for some of the bizarre features of the craft disappeared and it became almost conventional looking.

A longer nose was added that protruded more conventionally past the wing leading edge. The engine nacelles became more streamlined. The high cockpit greenhouse enclosure was reduced in height. Minor changes were made in an attempt to optimize the design. Detail filleting was cleaned up around the wing-fuselage juncture and the main gear doors.

At the Naval Aircraft Factory the landing gear was twice damaged during simulated carrier landing tests, on February 3 and May 18, 1942. The Naval Aircraft Factory repaired the damage both times. The Navy made a few more flights and then sent it back to Grumman for a general overhaul. The next flight took place on April 23, 1943. More flights and more gear collapses were in store for the craft; in fact, one collapse occurred while the ship was parked! And on December 11, 1944, a gear-up landing caused damage as the ship set down at the NAS, New York. As far as the Navy was concerned it was the last straw and the fuselage was taken for use in training fire crews.

The Skyrocket, at the end of its career, had made 211 flights with 155.7 hours of flight time without getting anyone's serious attention as a possible production item. Its main contribution to the Grumman lineup of fine fighters was the knowledge Grumman gained for use in the later design of the F7F Tigercat, a twin-engine single-place fighter that not only went into production at war's end but was a pretty hot ship to be reckoned with until the advent of the first jets. It should also be mentioned that Grumman tried to woo the USAF with a design similar to the F5F-1, the XP-50. It had a tricycle gear. The prototype XP-50 crashed on May 14, 1941.

After the F6F Hellcat (already discussed), the next Grumman fighter type was the F7F. It was also a twin-engine design, only this time quite conventional in layout except for the two huge engines pulling the relatively small, compact airframe through the air. The XF7F-1 was known as the Tigercat and, as a production aircraft, showed the way for both twin-engine layout and tricycle landing gears on carrier-based aircraft. Neither had been used operationally from a carrier's deck before.

Using two Pratt & Whitney R-2800's that were similar to those used on the Hellcat, the F7F weighed in at 22,560 pounds maximum

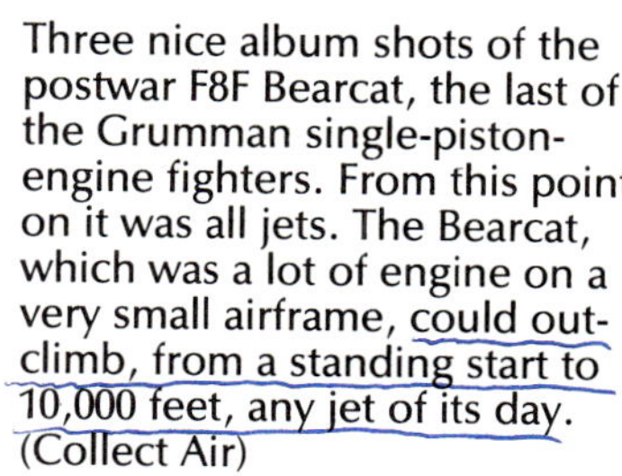

Three nice album shots of the postwar F8F Bearcat, the last of the Grumman single-piston-engine fighters. From this point on it was all jets. The Bearcat, which was a lot of engine on a very small airframe, could outclimb, from a standing start to 10,000 feet, any jet of its day. (Collect Air)

gross, a couple thousand pounds less than the weight of two Hellcats. The high power-to-weight ratio provided a top speed of 435 miles per hour at 22,200 feet and a blistering rate of climb of 4,520 feet per minute! The first flight of the prototype, initially powered with Wright R-2600-14's instead of the Pratt & Whitneys, took place in December 1943.

The plans for armament were awesome and were carried through to production aircraft. There were four fifty-caliber machine guns in the nose and four 20 mm aircraft cannon mounted in the wing roots. Four thousand rounds of ammunition fed the guns and, for good measure, the Tigercat also could carry two 1,000-pound bombs. Now *that was firepower*, and it could be carried over a range of 1,170 miles! The wings were short, broad and squared off at the tips. They spanned fifty-one feet six inches. Fuselage length was only forty-five feet 4½ inches, still down in the normal fighter plane size range.

After the first prototype crashed May 1, 1944, testing soon got underway again with the hurried arrival of a second machine. The Navy really liked the idea of so much firepower and envisioned the Marines raising havoc with the Japanese during ground attacks in island-hopping offensives. Grumman was given a contract for 500 F7F-1's; however, this was later curtailed as the war neared its end. It was at this point the 2,100 horsepower R-2800-22W powerplants were added to the package. For ultimate streamlining, big spinners were affixed to the propellers of the prototypes and the first few production aircraft. Cooling problems, however, soon called for their removal.

With the advent of airborne radar, night fighters were coming in vogue. They had been put in effect successfully with the Hellcat. To really do the job it seemed natural to take advantage of the new twin-engine fighter and make it a two-man night fighter. A new model with two seats became the F7F-2N and sixty-four were built with a radar dish supplanting the four fifty-caliber machine guns in the nose. The process took a long time, however, and by the time the Japanese surrendered in 1945 the Tigercat had still not been involved in a combat situation.

However, Grumman had been hard at work, and in March of that year an improved F7F-3 with more powerful engines was rolled from the plant. Production was restricted to only 189 aircraft. The new F7F-3 was again a single-place design and had its machine guns reinstated to the nose. Another sixty of the two-place radar-equipped night fighters were also produced during 1946. The total production of 263 Tigercats was not a waste for they served admirably during the early days of the Korean War in 1951.

The last of the propeller-driven "cats" was the fabulous Bearcat, the F8F. With the Hellcat generally doing a great job of knocking down Zeros in the high Pacific skies it still had trouble, at times, keeping up with the nimble little Japanese fighter during low-level encounters. Grumman once more addressed the specific problem facing the Navy and designed an aircraft that would have super maneuverability at low altitude and a fast rate of climb. Without so much as a mockup the Navy awarded Grumman a development contract for the new plane on November 27, 1943. It put its trust in Grumman and, predictably, the company didn't let it down.

On August 21, 1944, the XF8F-1 Bearcat took to the air for the first time—a mere ten months after contract approval! In another five months the soon-to-be-popular little fighter was rolling out the plant doors at Bethpage. It reached some Naval units before the war was over but never actually got to try its new wings in a combat situation. To show how much it liked the new plane the Navy increased the contract from the original twenty-three units to 2,023 before the first one even got in the air. Now that's confidence in a manufacturer! Another 4,000 were placed on order and General Motors was awarded a contract to build 1,876 F2M-1 and -2 aircraft, its version of the F8F Bearcat. All those orders were of course canceled when the war ended. Only 765 Bearcats were finished.

The Bearcat was light and fast, which led to some interesting events in its career even though it did not get into combat. During the late forties, the time of the jet fighter's arrival in the Navy's inventory, the Bearcat could still show who was boss in the climb department. From a standing start at the end of a runway the Bearcat could get to 10,000 feet faster than any fighter plane in the world, including the jets. Its unsurpassed performance in the piston-engine department culminated when Darryl Greenamyer set the world propeller-driven speed record in a highly modified Bearcat September 21, 1969. The speed was 483.041 miles per hour. The Bearcat also did a stint with the Navy's Blue Angels in the early postwar years making it a well-known crowd pleaser.

The Bearcat was relatively small in stature when compared with the burly Hellcat. The wing span was thirty-five feet ten inches and the short overall length only twenty-eight feet three inches. The wings, rather than folding back along the fuselage sides as with the Wildcat and Hellcat, folded upward and inward from a hinge line about two thirds of the way out from the wing root. The folding portion's tips had the unusual feature that they would be torn away if the aircraft's g loading went above nine. Explosive bolts assured that if only one tip came away the other could be literally blown off.

A testimony to the aircraft's fine performance may still be witnessed most Septembers at the Reno Air Races, where hopped-up Bearcats thrill the crowd and give other competitors a run for their money. With the Bearcat the Grumman organization came to the end of the line for piston-engined fighters. The jet age arrived and Grumman began work to become just as successful in designing and building fighters with the new-fangled turbojet.

Their new jet-propelled breed-of-cat first appeared on the firm's drawing boards in early 1946. Labeled the XF9F-1, it was to be powered by four Westinghouse J30 engines, each rated at 1,500 pounds of thrust. Like the first biplane F4F-1 that was dropped (to be born again as the Wildcat), the F9F-1 was dropped when it became apparent that a fighter propelled by four puny jets was *not* the way to go. It was back to the drawing board. This time the designers came up with a winner—the F9F-2 Panther. It was built in fairly large numbers and was developed from -2 through -7 versions. Being an early design, the Panther did not have the advantage of swept wings. Grumman incorporated that technology in the F-98, which appeared on September 20, 1951. The swept-wing version was then called the Cougar. Both the Panther and Cougar found themselves in the Korean War and each performed in combat with the typical Grumman style of excellence that had come to be expected of the firm's products.

But even the best win the green banana once in awhile and Grumman's turn came with the XF10F-1 Jaguar. It must be admitted that the aircraft had some really gutsy features. There was a variable-sweep wing for high-speed flight *plus* a variable-incidence ability for lower-speed takeoff and landing. Considering the level of aeronautical technology in the early fifties, one would have thought that the adjustable wing would have been enough of a problem. It wasn't. To add to the wing's complexity, the whole leading edge slid forward, thus becoming a monstrous slat. Further, the wings were equipped with spoilers on their top and bottom surfaces to induce roll, helping along some rather tiny ailerons at the wingtips.

In addition, Grumman went to a T-tail, but not just any T-tail. It was a super sweptback delta T-tail, mounted atop the vertical fin with a huge bullet-shaped housing. Attached to the front of the bullet-shaped housing was a smaller delta canard. The idea was that control column movement would move the canard, which in turn moved the bullet-shaped housing attached to the all-moving delta stabilizer. The whole cumbersome system was an attempt to alleviate the need for a power-boost system for control movement. Most all other manufacturers had gone to power-boost systems by that time.

To use all these advanced features to make up an aircraft, a fuselage was required also. Grumman provided a large portly structure housing a Westinghouse J40 fitted with an afterburner. The engine was rated at 7,000 pounds static thrust but never managed to get up to specification. The landing gear also was retracted into the fuselage belly, giving the craft a very narrow tread.

All this design complexity led to a big aircraft whose outspread wings spanned fifty feet seven inches and the length was an astounding

One of the last operational uses for the Bearcat was in the role of Beatle Bomb, the all-yellow target of the early Navy Blue Angels flight demonstration team. (Collect Air)

fifty-four feet five inches. It weighed in at 20,426 pounds empty and 27,451 pounds loaded. With all the weight, size and unusual features, added to the anemic engine, the program was destined to become a monumental flop.

While orders piled up during the design stage they were steadily (and wisely) withdrawn until, in the end, only two Jaguars were built. The first of thirty-two test flights of the number one machine was May 19, 1952. The other one never got off the ground. On June 12, 1952, the program was ended—too much was tried at the same time and each test seemed like a first flight. Both planes were used up in a nonflying manner. One was an artillery target, the other was smashed during landing barrier experiments.

If the Jaguar was all wrong the F11F-1 Tiger was all right. It was really a slimmed-down, lighter, more powerful Cougar. The new fighter was meant to compete supersonically with the Century Series fighters the USAF was developing. After a lot of teething problems the new aircraft was ready to join the fleet in March 1957.

A couple of interesting features of the Tiger were the area-ruled fuselage (the first for the Navy) and the full-span spoilers instead of ailerons. That allowed the entire trailing edge to be used for flaps. The maneuverable craft was a real hotshot at low-level subsonic speeds. Thousands of people became familiar with it during the great air shows put on by the Blue Angels during the late fifties. By 1959, however, they were removed from front-line duty, as newer and better fighters were on their way, particularly the McDonnell F4 Phantom II. The new F4 fighter was a truly high-performance aircraft of the first order and the Tiger was no match for it.

The next Grumman fighter, the XF12F-1, was a paper design to compete with the Phantom II. Never built, its claim to notoriety was the arrangement by which the crew entered the aircraft. The two seats were lowered through the fuselage bottom, the crew sat down and buckled up. The seats were then raised to a conventional position within the fuselage. It was all part of a supersonic escape capsule the craft was hoping to feature. The program was stopped while still in the planning stage, since Grumman engineering was, at the time, heavily involved in the design of the Navy version of the F-111A, the F-111B.

The last of the cat fighters (to date) is of course the current marvelous first-line naval fighter the F-14A Tomcat. Supersonic, heavily armed, all-weather and, due to the variable swept wing (thank you Jaguar), extremely maneuverable. It is without doubt the finest carrier fighter in the world today and probably tomorrow.

Yes, the cat had nine lives. Count them, Wildcat, Hellcat, Tigercat, Bearcat, Panther, Cougar, Jaguar, Tiger and Tomcat. However, the two most important, when viewed against the tapestry of history, have to be the Wildcat and Hellcat. Either one was produced in numbers far greater than the sum total of all the others combined. However, the real measure of their worth is the role they each played in first *stopping* the Japanese in the Pacific war, and then in turning it into a victory. No war before or since has put a burden on aircraft the likes of which was handled by the Wildcat and Hellcat. Indeed the admiral was right when he said, "The name Grumman on aircraft is like the name Sterling on silver."

WILDCAT/ HELLCAT FACT FILE

CHAPTER X

The material in this chapter is arranged to provide a concise source of dimensions, specifications and performance data for the Grumman F4F Wildcat and F6F Hellcat series of fighter airplanes. The aircraft are covered in chronological order by model of each type. Also included is a complete listing of the service serial numbers of the aircraft.

Grumman XF4F-1 (Model G-16)

First Flight: None
Number Built: None
USN BuAer Number: None issued
Span (upper and lower wings): 27 feet
Wing Area: 250 square feet
Length: 23 feet 3 inches
Height: 10 feet 10 inches
Powerplant: Wright XR-1670-02 14-cylinder twin-row radial air-cooled engine producing 850 horsepower at takeoff and 775 horsepower at 10,000 feet with single-stage/single-speed supercharger; or Pratt & Whitney XR-1830-92 Twin Wasp 14-cylinder twin-row radial air-cooled engine producing 875 horsepower at takeoff and 800 horsepower at 8,000 feet with single-stage/single-speed supercharger
Propeller: Hamilton Standard 3-blade controllable-pitch
Armament: One 30 and one 50 cal. Browning machine gun mounted in the nose
Empty Weight: 3,320 pounds
Gross Weight: 4,594 pounds
Maximum Speed: 264 miles per hour (est.) at 10,500 feet
Normal Range: 853 miles (est.)
Initial Climb Rate: 2,000 feet per minute (est.)
Service Ceiling: 29,400 feet (est.)
Wing Loading: 18 pounds per square foot
Power Loading: 5.6 pounds per horsepower
Airfoil: NACA 23012
The Grumman XF4F-1 was designed in response to a November 1935 BuAer competition for a new carrier fighter. By mid-summer of 1936 the biplane design was abandoned when it became evident it was no better than previous Grumman biplane fighters and not nearly as viable as the Brewster XF2A-1 Buffalo monoplane shipboard fighter, which was its direct competitor in the competition.

Grumman XF4F-2 Wildcat (Model G-18)

First Flight: September 2, 1937
Number Built: 1
USN BuAer Number: 0383
Span: 34 feet
Wing Area: 232 square feet
Length: 26 feet 5 inches
Height: 11 feet 11 inches
Powerplant: Pratt & Whitney R-1830-66 Twin Wasp 14-cylinder twin-row radial air-cooled engine producing 1,050 horsepower at takeoff and 900 horsepower at 12,000 feet with single-stage/single-speed supercharger
Propeller: Hamilton Standard 3-blade constant-speed; 10-foot diameter
Armament: Two 50 cal. Browning machine guns in nose with provision for additional two in wings. Also, wings had provision to carry two 100-pound bombs.
Empty Weight: 4,035 pounds
Gross Weight: 5,386 pounds
Maximum Speed: 290 miles per hour at 10,000 feet
Normal Range: 740 miles
Initial Climb Rate: 2,650 feet per minute
Service Ceiling: 27,400 feet

The Grumman XF4F-2 was the comeback for the firm after the -1 model was shown to be obsolete while still on the drawing board. The -2 design was started on August 28, 1936, as a monoplane. After flight tests, the aircraft was still short of performance when compared to the Brewster XF2A-1 Buffalo, its main competitor, and was therefore returned to the factory for modifications that resulted in the subsequent XF4F-3. Initial flights were conducted by test pilot Robert L. Hall, who had helped design and test the Gee Bee Model Z racer of the early thirties.

Grumman XF4F-3 Wildcat (Model G-36)

First Flight: February 12, 1939
Number Built: 1
USN BuAer Number: 0383
Span: 38 feet
Wing Area: 260 square feet
Length: 28 feet
Height: 11 feet 8 inches
Powerplant: Pratt & Whitney R-1830-76 Twin Wasp 14-cylinder twin-row radial air-cooled engine producing 1,200 horsepower at takeoff and 1,000 horsepower at 19,000 feet, with two-stage/two-speed supercharger
Propeller: Curtiss 3-blade constant-speed; 9-foot 9-inch diameter
Armament: Two 30 cal. Browning machine guns in nose and two 50 cal. Browning machine guns in wings
Empty Weight: 4,863 pounds
Gross Weight: 6,099 pounds
Maximum Speed: 333.5 miles per hour at 20,500 feet
Normal Range: 907 miles
Initial Climb Rate: 2,800 feet per minute
Service Ceiling: 33,500 feet

This aircraft, rebuilt from the XF4F-2 airframe, had an increased wing span, a larger vertical tail, a more powerful engine and other refinements such as smaller ailerons and increased dihedral. The wingtips were squared off, as were the tips of the tail surfaces, which became a Grumman trademark. The craft was flown with and without a propeller spinner. The improved design was successful and the Navy placed an order for production models on August 8, 1939, for an initial fifty-four F4F-3 fighters.

Grumman F4F-3 Wildcat (Model G-36)

First Flight: Feburary 1940
Number Built: 288
USN BuAer Number: 1844 through 1897 (54 units); 2512 through 2538 (27 units); 3856 through 3874 (19 units); 3970 through 4057 (88 units); 12230 through 12329 (100 units)
Span: 38 feet
Wing Area: 260 square feet
Length: 28 feet 9 inches
Height: 11 feet 11 inches
Powerplant: Pratt & Whitney R-1830-76 Twin Wasp 14-cylinder twin-row radial air-cooled engine producing 1,200 horsepower at takeoff and 1,000 horsepower at 19,000 feet. Engine was fitted with a two-stage/two-speed supercharger. Some engines used were -86's.
Propeller: Curtiss 3-blade constant-speed; 9-foot 9-inch diameter
Armament: First two aircraft in series were armed the same as the XF4F-3. Later aircraft were fitted with four 50 cal. machine guns in the wings. Aircraft could also carry two 100-pound bombs under the wings.
Empty Weight: 5,238 pounds
Gross Weight: 7,065 pounds
Maximum Gross Weight: 8,152 pounds
Maximum Speed: 328 miles per hour at 21,000 feet; 281 miles per hour at sea level
Normal Range: 860 miles
Initial Climb Rate: 2,300 feet per minute
Service Ceiling: 37,000 feet
These aircraft represented the first of the thousands of production Grumman F4F Wildcats that would see service with both the U.S. Navy and the Royal Navy of Great Britain throughout World War II.

Grumman F4F-3A Wildcat (Model G-36)

First Flight: Early 1941
Number Built: 95
USN BuAer Number: 3875 through 3969
Span: 38 feet
Wing Area: 260 square feet
Length: 28 feet 9 inches
Height: 11 feet 11 inches
Powerplant: Pratt & Whitney R-1830-90 Twin Wasp 14-cylinder twin-row radial air-cooled engine producing 1,200 horsepower at takeoff. Engine was fitted with single-stage/two-speed supercharger.
Propeller: Curtiss 3-blade constant-speed; 9-foot 9-inch diameter
Armament: Four 50 cal. machine guns in wings
Empty Weight: 5,216 pounds
Gross Weight: 6,876 pounds
Maximum Speed: 312 miles per hour at 16,000 feet
Normal Range: 825 miles
Initial Climb Rate: 2,430 feet per minute
Service Ceiling: 34,300 feet
These aircraft, while having less performance than the F4F-3, were built as a stopgap measure when it appeared that the Pratt & Whitney two-speed/two-stage supercharged R-1830-75 and -86 might be delayed. It was considered better to have this lesser performance aircraft than

The F4F-3S Wildcatfish.

none at all. The first thirty of these planes were delivered to the British as the Martlet III, with the balance going to the U.S. Navy and Marines. The first F3F-3A was delivered to VMF-111 on April 10, 1941.

Grumman F4F-3P Wildcat (Model G-36)

First Flight: Unknown
Number Built: Unknown
USN BuAer Numbers: (known examples) 2512, 2517, 2524, 2526, 2530, 2537
Specifications were generally the same as the Grumman F4F-3 model except aircraft were fitted for photo-reconnaissance missions. The exact number of conversions is not known.

Grumman F4F-3S Wildcatfish (Model G-36)

First Flight: February 28, 1943
Number Built: 1
USN BuAer Number: 4039
Span: 38 feet
Wing Area: 260 square feet
Length: 39 feet 1 inch
Height: 18 feet 1¾ inches
Powerplant: Pratt & Whitney R-1830-76 Twin Wasp 14-cylinder twin-row radial air-cooled engine providing 1,200 horsepower at takeoff and 1,000 horsepower at 19,000 feet. Engine had two-stage/two-speed supercharger.
Propeller: Curtiss 3-blade constant speed; 9-foot 9-inch diameter
Armament: Four 50 cal. machine guns in wings with 800 rounds per gun
Empty Weight: 5,804 pounds
Gross Weight: 7,506 pounds
Maximum Speed: 266 miles per hour at 20,300 feet

Normal Range: 600 miles at 132 miles per hour
Initial Climb Rate: 2,460 feet per minute
Service Ceiling: 33,500 feet
Both the designation F4F-3S and "Wildcatfish" were unofficial. The transformation to a floatplane was made by the Edo Corporation using two model 62-6560 floats along with a small fin on either end of the stabilizer to counteract the forward wetted surface of the floats. These were later supplemented by means of a fin beneath the aft fuselage. One hundred of these floatplane versions were on order but all were canceled after the prototype was built. It was determined there was no real use for them.

Grumman XF4F-4 Wildcat (Model G-36)

First Flight: April 1941
Number Built: 1
USN BuAer Number: 1897
Span: 38 feet
Wing Area: 260 square feet
Length: 28 feet 9 inches
Height: 11 feet 11 inches
Powerplant: Pratt & Whitney R-1830-76 Twin Wasp 14-cylinder twin-row radial air-cooled engine producing 1,200 horsepower at takeoff and 1,000 horsepower at 19,000 feet. Engine was fitted with two-stage/two-speed supercharger.
Propeller: Curtiss 3-blade constant-speed; 9-foot 9-inch diameter
Armament: Four 50 cal. machine guns in wings
Empty Weight: 5,776 pounds
Gross Weight: 7,489 pounds
Maximum Speed: 326 miles per hour at 19,500 feet
Normal Range: Unknown
Initial Climb Rate: 1,900 feet per minute
Service Ceiling: 34,000 feet
This was the first of the Grumman Wildcat series to feature folding wings which reduced the span for aircraft carrier storage from thirty-eight feet to fourteen feet four inches. The folding operation was performed hydraulically. The weight of the mechanism was considered to be excessive for its function and the system after this one aircraft was converted to the manual mode on subsequent F4F-4 fighters.

Grumman F4F-4 Wildcat (Model G-36)

First Flight: November 1941
Number Built: 1,169
USN BuAer Numbers: 4058 through 4098 (41 units); 5030 through 5049 (20 units); 5050 through 5262 (213 units); 01991 through 02152 (162 units); 03385 through 03544 (160 units); 11655 through 12227 (573 units)
Span: 38 feet
Wing Area: 260 square feet
Length: 28 feet 9 inches
Height: 11 feet 9 inches
Powerplant: Pratt & Whitney R-1830-86 Twin Wasp 14-cylinder twin-row radial air-cooled engine producing 1,200 horsepower at takeoff and 1,000 horsepower at 19,000 feet. Engine was fitted with two-stage/two-speed supercharger.
Propeller: Curtiss 3-blade constant-speed; 9-foot 9-inch diameter
Armament: Six 50 cal. machine guns in wings
Empty Weight: 5,758 pounds

Gross Weight: 7,964 pounds
Maximum Speed: 318 miles per hour at 19,400 feet; 275 miles per hour at sea level
Normal Range: 770 miles
Initial Climb Rate: 2,190 feet per minute
Service Ceiling: 33,700 feet
These F4F-4 Wildcats had folding wings, manually operated, that more than doubled the number of aircraft that could be carried aboard a carrier. They also had self-sealing fuel tanks and armor plating. This, along with hard spots for drop tanks or two 100-pound bombs under the wings, made it a real competitor in the South Pacific war. Eight cowl flaps aided the engine in cooling.

Grumman F4F-4A Wildcat (Model G-36)

First Flight: None
Number Built: None
USN BuAer Number: None issued
The F4F-4A was to be fitted with the Pratt & Whitney R-1830-90 engine. It became a design project only and none were constructed.

Grumman F4F-4B Wildcat (Model G-36)

This was the U.S. Navy designation for the Lend-Lease Wildcat IV. See that aircraft in Fact File for data on performance and specifications. The craft was also called the Martlet IV.

Grumman F4F-4P Wildcat (Model G-36)

First Flight: Unknown
Number Built: 1 (known)
USN BuAer Number: 03386
This was an F4F-4 converted to use as a photo-recon-mission aircraft. Whether more than one conversion was made is unknown.

Grumman XF4F-5 Wildcat (Model G-36)

First Flight: June 1940
Number Built: 2
USN BuAer Numbers: 1846 and 1847
Span: 38 feet
Wing Area: 260 square feet
Length: 28 feet 10 inches
Height: 11 feet 10 inches
Powerplant: Wright R-1820-40 Cyclone 9-cylinder single-row radial air-cooled engine producing 1,200 horsepower at takeoff. Engine was fitted with single-stage/two-speed supercharger. Further engine changes were made later: 1846 was fitted with a Wright R-1820-54 with a turbo-supercharger and 1847 was fitted with a Wright XR-1820-48 with a two-stage supercharger installed. Test results showed 1846 capable of 340 miles per hour at 26,400 feet and 1847 with a lesser speed of 316 miles per hour at 19,300 feet.
Propeller: Hamilton Standard 3-blade constant-speed
Armament: None fitted
Empty Weight: 4,887 pounds
Gross Weight: 6,063 pounds
Maximum Speed: 306 miles per hour at 15,000 feet
Normal Range: Unknown
Initial Climb Rate: 2,350 feet per minute
Service Ceiling: 35,500 feet
These two aircraft, the third and fourth F4F-3's, were used to evaluate the possibility of using the Wright single-row radials instead of the twin-row Pratt & Whitney radials.

Grumman XF4F-6 Wildcat (Model G-36)

First Flight: October 1940
Number Built: 1
USN BuAer Number: 7031
Span: 38 feet
Wing Area: 260 square feet
Length: 28 feet 9 inches
Height: 11 feet 10 inches
Powerplant: Pratt & Whitney R-1830-90 Twin-Wasp 14-cylinder twin-row radial air-cooled engine producing 1,200 horsepower at takeoff and 1,000 horsepower at 11,000 feet. A single-stage/two-speed supercharger was used.
Propeller: Curtiss 3-blade constant-speed
Armament: None fitted
Empty Weight: 4,985 pounds
Gross Weight: 7,065 pounds
Maximum Speed: 319 miles per hour at 16,100 feet
Normal Range: Unknown
Initial Climb Rate: 2,600 feet per minute
Service Ceiling: 34,000 feet
This aircraft was ordered by the Navy to evaluate the less complex Pratt & Whitney R-1830-90 engine at a time when development problems were being encountered with the R-1830-76 and -86 engines.

Grumman F4F-7 Wildcat (Model G-36)

First Flight: December 30, 1941
Number Built: 21
USN BuAer Numbers: 5263 through 5283
Span: 38 feet
Wing Area: 260 square feet
Length: 29 feet 10 inches
Height: 11 feet 9 inches
Powerplant: Pratt & Whitney R-1830-86 Twin Wasp 14-cylinder twin-row radial air-cooled engine producing 1,200 horsepower at takeoff and 1,000 horsepower at 19,000 feet. Engine was fitted with two-stage/two-speed supercharger.
Propeller: Curtiss 3-blade constant-speed
Armament: None fitted
Empty Weight: 5,456 pounds
Gross Weight: 10,328 pounds (with 555 gallons of fuel)
Maximum Speed: 310 miles per hour at 19,400 feet
Normal Range: 3,700 miles
Initial Climb Rate: 1,765 feet per minute
Service Ceiling: 26,900 feet
These long range photo-recon aircraft featured auto-pilots, nonfolding wings and camera installation in the rear fuselage. The additional length was the result of fuel dump outlets that extended rearward below the rudder. To use up the tremendous fuel load at maximum range flying speed required nearly twenty-four hours of straight flying time! Armor plate was deleted on these aircraft which were later converted to F4F-4's.

Grumman XF4F-8 Wildcat (Model G-36)

First Flight: November 8, 1942
Number Built: 2
USN BuAer Numbers: 12228 and 12229
Span: 38 feet

Wildcats in formation above the clouds in late 1943. (U.S. Navy)

Wing Area: 260 square feet
Length: 28 feet 10 inches
Height: 11 feet 9 inches
Powerplant: Wright XR-1820-56 Cyclone 9-cylinder single-row radial air-cooled engine producing 1,350 horsepower at takeoff. Engine was fitted with single-stage/two-speed supercharger.
Propeller: Hamilton Standard 3-blade constant-speed
Armament: Four 50 cal. wing guns
Empty Weight: 5,365 pounds
Gross Weight: 7,080 pounds
Maximum Speed: 321 miles per hour at 16,800 feet
Normal Range: Unknown
Initial Climb Rate: 3,125 feet per minute
Service Ceiling: 36,400 feet
These two aircraft were prototypes for the General Motors Eastern Aircraft Division FM-1 Wildcats. They were intended to be light in weight and were initially fitted with slotted flaps before reverting to split flaps. Aircraft number 12229 was later fitted with the larger fin used on the General Motors FM-2. This was required to counteract the increased horsepower used on these aircraft during takeoff and carrier waveoffs during landings. The oil cooler, which had been under the left wing, was relocated in the engine compartment.

General Motors FM-1 Wildcat

First Flight: September 1, 1942
Number Built: 1,060
USN BuAer Numbers: 14992 through 15951 (960 units); 46738 through 46837 (100 units)
Span: 38 feet
Wing Area: 260 square feet
Length: 28 feet 10 inches

Height: 11 feet 9 inches
Powerplant: Pratt & Whitney R-1830-86 Twin Wasp 14-cylinder twin-row radial air-cooled engine producing 1,200 horsepower at takeoff and 1,000 horsepower at 19,000 feet. Engine was fitted with two-stage/two-speed supercharger.
Propeller: Curtiss 3-blade constant speed; 9-foot 9-inch diameter
Armament: Four 50 cal. machine guns in wings; two 100-pound bombs or six 5-inch rockets under the wings
Empty Weight: 5,895 pounds
Gross Weight: 7,975 pounds
Maximum Gross Weight: 8,762 pounds
Maximum Speed: 320 miles per hour at 18,800 feet; 284 miles per hour at sea level. (Economical cruise speed was 162 miles per hour.)
Normal Range: 830 miles
Maximum Range: 1,275 miles
Initial Climb Rate: 3,300 feet per minute
Service Ceiling: 34,000 feet
With the design advent of the Grumman F6F Hellcat, the Grumman Company had to get rid of the Wildcat as a production item. The Wildcat, though a sturdy, well-designed fighter, was still not up to a one-on-one combat situation with the nimble Japanese Zero. The Hellcat was. General Motors was ready to take up the slack with five East Coast factories that had previously turned out automobiles. These factories formed the Eastern Aircraft Division on January 21, 1942, and off they went, producing fighter planes and torpedo bombers pell-mell just as they had done automobiles in the prewar years. The FM-1 was built at the Linden, New Jersey, plant—still in existence, and still trying to stem a Japanese tide (this time cars) as it did forty years ago. One of these aircraft is on display at the National Air and Space Museum (15392 restored by Grumman), and the famous Wildcat lives on—for 100 years at least, as that is what a restored aircraft at that museum is supposed to do.

General Motors FM-2 Wildcat

First Flight: 1943
Number Built: 4,777
USN BuAer Number: 15952 through 16791 (840 units); 46838 through 47437 (600 units); 55050 through 55649 (600 units); 56684 through 57083 (400 units); 73499 through 75158 (1660 units); 86297 through 86973 (677 units); 86974 through 87719 canceled
Span: 38 feet
Wing Area: 260 square feet
Length: 28 feet 10.6 inches
Height: 11 feet 9 inches
Powerplant: Wright R-1820-56 Cyclone 9-cylinder single-row radial air-cooled engine producing 1,350 horsepower at takeoff. A single-stage/two-speed supercharger was fitted. Also used was the -56W.
Propeller: Curtiss 3-blade constant-speed
Armament: Four 50 cal. machine guns in wings; six 5-inch rockets under wings (last 826 aircraft)
Empty Weight: 5,448 pounds
Gross Weight: 7,487 pounds
Maximum Weight: 8,271 pounds
Maximum Speed: 332 miles per hour at 28,800 feet; 306 miles per hour at sea level (Economical cruise speed was 164 miles per hour.)
Normal Range: 900 miles
Maximum Range: 1,310 miles

Initial Climb Rate: 3,650 feet per minute
Service Ceiling: 34,700 feet
This type was the most widely produced of any of the Wildcat variants. The feature most noted on the last 826 FM-2's were the higher rudder and vertical fin that were required due to the increased horsepower of the water-injected Wright 1820-56W that produced 1,350 horsepower at takeoff. These aircraft were also the same as the Wildcat VI produced for Great Britain.

Grumman Martlet Mk. I (Model G-36A)

First Flight: May 10, 1940
Number Built: 82
Royal Navy Serial Numbers: AL231 through AL262 (32 units)
AX725 through AX747 (23 units)
BJ554 through BJ570 (17 units)
BT447 through BT456 (10 units)
(The above eighty-two aircraft were originally destined for the French Navy.)
AX753 through AX754 (2 units)
AX761 (1 unit)
AX824 through AX829 (6 units)
BJ507 thourgh BJ527 (21 units)
(The above thirty aircraft were originally built as F4F-3's and assigned USN BuAer numbers 3875 through 3904. They were intended for delivery to Greece.)
Span: 38 feet
Wing Area: 260 square feet
Length: 28 feet 10 inches
Height: 11 feet 9 inches
Powerplant: Wright GR-1820-G205A Cyclone 9-cylinder single-row radial air-cooled engine producing 1,200 horsepower at takeoff. A single-stage/two-speed supercharger was fitted.
Propeller: Hamilton Standard 3-blade constant speed
Armament: Four 50 cal. machine guns in wings
Empty Weight: 4,887 pounds
Gross Weight: 6,063 pounds
Maximum Speed: 306 miles per hour at 15,000 feet
Normal Range: Unknown
Initial Rate of Climb: 2,350 feet per minute
Service Ceiling: 35,500 feet
These aircraft, with nonfolding wings, were ordered by the French government and assumed by the British Purchasing Commission after the fall of France. The first victory for the Martlet was December 25, 1940, when it shot down a German Junkers Ju-88. These aircraft were later renamed Wildcat Mk. I. One still exists on display at Yeovilton, England.

Grumman Martlet Mk. II (Model G-36A)

First Flight: October 1, 1940
Number Built: 90
Royal Navy Serial Numbers: AJ100 through AJ153 (54 units); AM964 through AM999 (36 units)
Span: 38 feet
Wing Area: 260 square feet
Length: 29 feet 1 inch
Height: 11 feet 9 inches

Powerplant: Pratt & Whitney R-1830-S3C-4G Twin Wasp 14-cylinder twin-row radial air-cooled engine producing 1,200 horsepower at takeoff. Engine was fitted with a single-stage/two-speed supercharger.
Propeller: Curtiss 3-blade constant-pitch
Armament: Four (first 10 aircraft), and later six 50 cal. machine guns in wings
Empty Weight: 5,345 pounds
Gross Weight: 7,512 pounds
Maximum Speed: 293 miles per hour at 13,000 feet
Normal Range: 890 miles
Initial Rate of Climb: Unknown
Service Ceiling: 31,000 feet
Except for the first ten aircraft the balance of the Martlet II's had folding wings. Folded span was fourteen feet four inches. Aircraft designation later reverted to Wildcat Mk. II.

Grumman Martlet Mk. III (Model G-36)

First Flight: 1941
Number Built: 10
Royal Navy Serial Numbers: AM954 through AM963
These aircraft were the same as the Grumman F4F-3A Wildcats and were en route to Greece when that nation fell to the Axis. The aircraft were taken over by the British at Gibraltar and designated Martlet III's. That designation was later changed to Wildcat III.

Grumman Martlet Mk. IV (Model G-36)

First Flight: 1942
Number Built: 220
Royal Navy Serial Numbers: FN100 through FN319
Span: 38 feet
Wing Area: 260 square feet
Length: 28 feet 5 inches
Height: 11 feet 9 inches
Powerplant: Wright R-1820-40B Cyclone 9-cylinder single-row radial air-cooled engine producing 1,200 horsepower at takeoff. Engine was fitted with single-stage/two-speed supercharger.
Propeller: Hamilton Standard 3-blade constant-speed
Armament: Six 50 cal. machine guns in wings
Empty Weight: 5,773 pounds
Gross Weight: 7,904 pounds
Maximum Speed: 298 miles per hour at 14,000 feet
Normal Range: Unknown
Initial Climb Rate: Unknown
Service Ceiling: 30,100 feet
These were the last Wildcats built for the British by Grumman as the design was turned over to General Motors and became the FM-1. The machine guns on these aircraft were British M-53A Brownings. These aircraft were also designated F4F-4B but no USN Serials were issued for them. Like the other Martlets, these aircraft were redesignated Wildcat IV by the British.

General Motors Martlet V/Wildcat V

First Flight: 1942
Number Built: 312
Royal Navy Serial Numbers: JV325 through JV636
Dimensions and specifications for these aircraft are the same as those given for the General Motors FM-1 Wildcat.

General Motors Martlet VI/Wildcat VI

First Flight: 1944
Number Built: 370
Royal Navy Serial Numbers: JV637 through JV924 (288 units); JW785 through JW836 (52 units); JZ860 through JZ889 (30 units)
Dimensions and specifications for these aircraft are the same as those given for the General Motors FM-2 Wildcat. Ninety-five of the aircraft were originally issued USN BuAer numbers before the planes were turned over to Great Britain.

Grumman XF6F-1 Hellcat

First Flight: June 26, 1942
Number Built: 1
USN BuAer Number: 02981 (02982 was also issued, but not used for -1)
Span: 42 feet 10 inches
Wing Area: 334 square feet
Length: 33 feet 7 inches
Height: 11 feet 3 inches
Powerplant: Wright R-2600-16 Cyclone 14-cylinder twin-row radial air-cooled engine producing 1,600 horsepower at takeoff and 1,200 horsepower at altitude
Propeller: Curtiss Electric 3-blade with cuffs and spinner
Armament: Six 50 cal. Browning M.6 machine guns mounted in the wings with 400 rounds per gun
Performance Data: Not established due to curtailment of this model
After completion and early testing it was decided that while the XF6F-1 was a major gain in aircraft performance over the Wildcat, its abilities could be increased still further by changing over to the more powerful Pratt & Whitney R-2800 series Double Wasp engine.

Grumman XF6F-2 Hellcat

First Flight: January 7, 1944
Number Built: 1
USN BuAer Number: 66244
Span: 42 feet 10 inches
Wing Area: 334 square feet
Length: 33 feet 7 inches
Height: 11 feet 3 inches
Powerplant: Pratt & Whitney R-2800-21 Double Wasp 18-cylinder twin-row radial air-cooled engine fitted with a Birman turbo-supercharger
Propeller: Hamilton Standard Hydromatic 3-blade
Armament: Six 50 cal. machine guns located in wings
Performance Data: Not established due to curtailment of this model
This aircraft, while proposed at the same time as the XF6F-1 and XF6F-3 models, did not get into the air until much later. It represented an attempt to increase the Hellcat's performance by turbo-supercharging the initially fitted Wright R-2600-15 and then, the later Pratt & Whitney engine listed above. Either engine improved the aircraft's performance at 20,000 feet to that of sea level. The project was dropped due to fire danger from the supercharger pumping gasoline into the engine's exhaust.

Grumman XF6F-3 Hellcat

First Flight: July 30, 1942
Number Built: 2
USN BuAer Number: 02982 (02981 was later converted to -3)
Span: 42 feet 10 inches

Wing Area: 334 square feet
Length: 33 feet 7 inches
Height: 11 feet 3 inches
Powerplant: Pratt & Whitney R-2800-10 Double Wasp 18-cylinder twin-row radial air-cooled engine producing 2,000 horsepower at takeoff and 1,975 horsepower at 16,900 feet
Propeller: Curtiss Electric 3-blade with cuffs and spinner
Armament: Six 50 cal. Colt-Browning machine guns in wings
Empty Weight: 9,042 pounds
Gross Weight: 11,381 pounds
Maximum Speed: 380 miles per hour at 23,400 feet; 315 miles per hour at sea level
Range: 1,090 miles (1,590 with external drop tank)
Initial Rate of Climb: 3,500 feet per minute
Service Ceiling: 38,400 feet
The XF6F-3 was the final prototype of the F6F-3 production aircraft. The XF6F-1 was, after an engine change to the Pratt & Whitney, brought up to XF6F-3 standards. The two aircraft were then used for flight testing of the new Hellcat fighter.

Grumman F6F-3 Hellcat

First Flight: October 4, 1942
Number Built: 4,402 (4,397 units listed below; other 5 serials unknown)
USN BuAer Numbers: 04775 through 04958 (184 units); 08798 through 09047 (244 units); 25721 through 26195 (475 units); 39999 through 43137 (3,139 units); 65890 through 66244 (355 units)
Serial Number Note: 66244 was finished as the XF6F-2 but was later delivered as XF6F-3 43137.
Span: 42 feet 10 inches
Wing Area: 344 square feet
Length: 33 feet 7 inches
Height: 11 feet 1 inch
Powerplant: Pratt & Whitney R-2800-10 Double Wasp 18-cylinder twin-row radial air-cooled engine producing 2,000 horsepower at takeoff and 1,975 horsepower at 16,900 feet
Propeller: Hamilton Standard 3-blade full feathering
Armament: Six 50 cal. Colt-Browning machine guns in wings
Empty Weight: 9,023 pounds
Gross Weight: 12,415 pounds
Maximum Speed: 388 miles per hour at 25,000 feet; 312 miles per hour at sea level
Normal Range: 1,085 miles
Initial Climb Rate: 3,650 feet per minute
Service Ceiling: 35,500 feet
These aircraft, the first production batch, had the same performance and dimensions as the XF6F-3 prototypes listed above. The main differences were the smaller redesigned landing gear fairings, a three-bladed Hamilton Standard propeller with no spinner and a provision for the ventral drop tank. Other changes made as the production series continued were streamlined gun fairings, the deletion of the lower cowl flaps, and a straight aerial mast.

Grumman F6F-3E Hellcat

These Hellcats were the night-fighting version of the aircraft. Eighteen F6F-3E's were constructed with the main differences being the AN/APS-4 radar pod slung under the right wing. Specifications and dimensions were the same as the parent F6F-3.

Grumman XF6F-3N Hellcat

The XF6F-3N was a single F6F-3 converted to a night fighter using the AN/APS-6 faired wing-mounted radar dome. It made for a more streamlined installation than that used on the F6F-3E aircraft. This plane was the prototype for the F6F-3N, of which 205 copies were built. Specifications and dimensions were the same as the parent F6F-3.

Grumman F6F-3N Hellcat

These 205 aircraft were night fighters fitted with the streamlined AN/APS-6 randome faired into the right wing. Other changes included the installation of the 2,200 horsepower Pratt & Whitney R-2800-10W engine and flat-fronted windshields for better visibility. Other specifications and dimensions were the same as those of the F6F-3 parent design.

Grumman XF6F-4 Hellcat

The XF6F-1 prototype (BuAer 02981) was rebuilt as the sole XF6F-4. The major object of the program was to show the installation of four 20 mm aircraft cannon mounted in the wings with 200 rounds of ammunition per gun. In addition, a Pratt & Whitney R-2800-27 was installed for improved performance. After testing, it was decided not to produce the F6F-4 and the plane was once more converted—this time to F6F-3 standards—and delivered to the Navy for routine fighter use.

Grumman F6F-5 Hellcat

First Flight: April 4, 1944
Number Built: 7,870 (an additional 628 were canceled)
USN BuAer Numbers: 58000 through 58999 (1,000 units); 69992 through 72991 (3,000 units); 77259 through 80258 (3,000 units); 93652 through 94521 (870 units); canceled serials: 94522 through 94751 (230 units); 111349 through 111748 (400 units)
Span: 42 feet 10 inches
Wing Area: 344 square feet
Length: 33 feet 7 inches
Height: 11 feet 1 inch
Powerplant: Pratt & Whitney R-2800-10W Double Wasp 18-cylinder twin-row radial air-cooled engine producing 2,000 horsepower at takeoff and 1,975 horsepower at 16,900 feet
Propeller: Hamilton Standard Hydromatic
Armament: Two 20 mm cannons and four 50 cal. machine guns in the wings or six 50 cal. machine guns in the wings. Also, provisions were made for carrying six 5-inch HVAR rockets under the wings or two 1,000-pound bombs under the fuselage.
Empty Weight: 9,238 pounds
Gross Weight: 12,483 pounds
Maximum Speed: 400 miles per hour at 20,000 feet; 318 miles per hour at sea level
Range: 1,300 miles (1,530 with drop tank)
Initial Rate of Climb: 3,200 feet per minute
Service Ceiling: 36,000 feet
The F6F-5 was an improved version of the Hellcat that featured a strengthened airframe, a smoother, closer-fitting cowl, flat-fronted windshield, spring tab ailerons, windows aft of the sliding canopy removed (on most models) and the provisions for the underwing ordnance listed above.

Grumman F6F-5K Hellcat

These aircraft were F6F-5 and F6F-5N's converted to radio-control target drones. Several were converted but the exact number is unknown.

Grumman F6F-5N Hellcat (also F6F-5E)

These radar-equipped night-fighter versions of the F6F-5 were built in large quantities, 1,529 with an additional 1,050 canceled. BuAer numbers for those built were 71463 through 72991. The canceled BuAer numbers were 108226 through 109272. In addition, several F6F-5's were also converted to F6F-5N's and included BuAer 93679, 94338 and 94473. The F6F-5N aircraft were fitted with AN/APS-6 radar pods faired into the right wing while the F6F-5E aircraft carried the AN/APS-4 units mounted under the right wing. Many of these aircraft carried the two 20 mm cannon plus four 50 cal. machine gun package of wing armament.

Grumman F6F-5P Hellcat

The specifications and performance of these aircraft were identical to the F6F-5 except they were fitted with a camera installed in the rear fuselage.

Grumman F6F-6 Hellcat

Two F6F-6's were built to explore the use of a four-bladed Hamilton Standard propeller coupled with a more powerful Pratt & Whitney R-2800-18W engine that produced 2,100 horsepower. The first of the two examples was first flown July 6, 1944, but no production was undertaken. Top speed was 417 miles per hour at 22,000 feet. Serial numbers of the two aircraft were BuAer 70188 and 70913. Other than the propeller and engine, the planes were stock F6F-5's.

Grumman Hellcat Mk. I (Gannet I)

These 252 aircraft were the F6F-3 sent to Great Britain under Lend-Lease. They originally carried USN BuAer numbers. The following is a listing of the Royal Navy serials as well as the corresponding BuAer numbers:

Royal Navy	*BuAer*
FN320 through FN329	04850 through 04859 (10 units)
FN330 through FN339	04945 through 04954 (10 units)
FN340 through FN349	08894 through 08903 (10 units)
FN350 through FN359	08954 through 08963 (10 units)
FN360 through FN369	09029 through 09038 (10 units)
FN370 through FN379	25778 through 25787 (10 units)
FN380 through FN389	25868 through 25877 (10 units)
FN390 through FN399	25958 through 25967 (10 units)
FN400 through FN409	26053 through 26062 (10 units)
FN410 through FN419	26148 through 26157 (10 units)
FN420 through FN429	65962 through 65971 (10 units)
FN430 through FN439	66082 through 66091 (10 units)
FN440 through FN449	66222 through 66231 (10 units)
JV100 through JV221	(122 units)

Grumman Hellcat Mk. II

These 925 aircraft were F6F-5's sent to Great Britain under Lend-Lease. They originally carried USN BuAer numbers. The following is a listing of the Royal Navy serials as well as the corresponding BuAer numbers:

Royal Navy	*BuAer*
JV222 through JV234	58220 through 58232 (13 units)
JV235 through JV297	58733 through 58795 (63 units)
JV298 through JV301	58966 through 58999 (4 units)
JV302 through JV324	69992 through 70014 (23 units)
JW700 through JW722	70015 through 70037 (23 units)
JW723 through JW772	70238 through 70287 (50 units)
JW773 through JW784	70463 through 70474 (12 units)
JW857 through JW894	70475 through 70512 (38 units)
JW895 through JW899	70688 through 70692 (5 units)
JX670 through JX739	70693 through 70762 (70 units)
JX740 through JX814	71163 through 71237 (75 units)
JX815 through JX889	71638 through 71712 (75 units)
JX890 through JX964	72113 through 72187 (75 units)
JX965 through JX967	72989 through 72991 (3 units)
JX968 through JX999 (32 units)	
JZ775 through JX827 (53 units)	
JZ890 through JZ999 (110 units)	
KD108 through KD160 (53 units)	
KE118 through KE265 (148 units)	

In addition to the above the following 76 aircraft were night fighters delivered as NF.II's (F6F-5N):

JX965 through JX967 (3 units)
JZ890 through JZ911 (22 units)
JZ947 through JZ959 (13 units)
JZ965 through JZ967 (3 units)
JZ995 through JZ999 (5 units)
KD108 through KD117 (10 units)
KD153 through KD157 (5 units)
KE160 through KE169 (10 units)
KE215 through KE219 (5 units)

Others were converted to FR.II's with a camera mounted in the rear fuselage.

APPENDIX TO FACT FILE

While it was not built by the Grumman Aircraft Engineering Corporation, the Japanese Mitsubishi Zero-Sen fighter was the primary adversary of both the Wildcat and the later Hellcat. With this in mind, and for the sake of comparison, the following data is presented for that fighter.

Mitsubishi A6M6C Model 53C Zero-Sen

First Flight: April 1, 1939
Span: 36 feet 1 inch
Wing Area: 229.271 square feet
Length: 29 feet 9 inches
Height: 9 feet 2 inches
Powerplant: Nakajima NK1P Sakae 31 14-cylinder twin-row air-cooled radial engine producing 1,120 horsepower at takeoff and 1,055 horsepower at 20,400 feet
Propeller: Constant-speed 3-blade
Armament: Two Type 99 (Oerlikon) 20 mm cannon and two 13.2 mm machine guns in wings and one 7.7 mm machine gun in engine cowling

This side view of the A6M2 shows off the very slender fuselage that faired back to the streamlined tail cone in an almost straight line. (Author Collection)

Empty Weight: 3,920 pounds
Gross Weight: 6,026 pounds (maximum weight, 6,508 pounds)
Maximum Speed: 346 miles per hour at 19,680 feet; 289 miles per hour at sea level
Range: 1,130 miles at 152 miles per hour
Initial Rate of Climb: 3,140 feet per minute
Service Ceiling: 35,100 feet
There were several models of the Zero, including even a floatplane fighter. Detailed analysis of the Zero is outside the scope of this book; however, the above data is representative of what that aircraft could accomplish. In all, a grand total of the various models came to 10,938 aircraft produced.

Addendum

The Hellcat was used for a time in 1945 by the French Flotille 1, Aeronavale, French Indochina, and as late as 1958 by the Uruguayan Servicio Aeronautica de la Marina. In both cases the numbers involved were few, eight or ten aircraft.

BIBLIOGRAPHY

Air Progress. New York, New York, monthly 1953 to 1975.

Andrade, John M., *U.S. Military Aircraft Designations and Serials Since 1909*. Midland Countries Publications, England, 1979.

Bowers, Peter M. and Swanborough, Gordon. *United States Navy Aircraft Since 1911*. Funk and Wagnalls, New York, New York, 1968.

Casey, Louis S. and Batchelor, John. *Naval Aircraft 1939–1945*. Phoebus Publishing Co., England, 1975.

Green, William. *Fighters, Volume Four; Warplanes of the Second World War*. Macdonald & Company, London, 1961.

Green, William. *Famous Fighters of the Second World War—Volume Two*. Doubleday and Company, Garden City, New York, 1962.

Hill, Richard M. *Grumman F6F-3/5 Hellcat*. Arco Publishing Company, New York, New York, 1971.

Horikoshi, Jiro. *Eagles of Mitsubishi*. University of Washington Press, 1981.

Jones, Floyd S. *U.S. Naval Fighters*. Aero Publishers, Fallbrook, California, 1977.

Kohn, Leo J. *Grumman F6F "Hellcat"—Pilots Flight Operating Instructions*. Aviation Publications, Appleton, Wisconsin, 1975.

Kohn, Leo J. *Pilots Handbook for Grumman Wildcat*. Aviation Publications, Appleton, Wisconsin, 1978.

Matt, Paul R. and Robinson, Bruce. *United States Navy and Marine Corps Fighters 1918–1962*. Aero Publishers, Fallbrook, California, 1962.

Mayborn, Mitch, et al. *Grumman Guidebook*. Flying Enterprise Publications, Dallas, Texas, 1976.

Mizrahi, J. V. *Carrier Fighters*. Sentry Books, Northridge, California, 1969.

Munson, Kenneth. *Fighters—Attack and Training Aircraft 1939–1945*. The Macmillian Co., New York, New York, 1969.

Nye, Willis L. *Masterplan Book #3*. Air Age Inc., New York, New York, 1963.

Okumiya, M., Horikoshi, J., and Caiden, M. *Zero*. Zenger Publishing Company, Inc., Washington, D.C., 1979.

Simmons, Walter. *Joe Foss—Flying Marine*. Zenger Publishing Company, Inc., Washington, D.C., 1979.

Sullivan, Jim. *F6F Hellcat in Action*. Squadron/Signal Publications, Carrollton, Texas, 1979.

Thetford, Owen. *British Naval Aircraft 1912–1958*. Putnam, London, 1958.

Tillman, Barrett. *Hellcat—The F6F in World War II*. Naval Institute Press, Annapolis, Maryland, 1979.

Wagner, Ray. *American Combat Planes*. Hanover House, Garden City, New York, 1960.

Wings and Airpower. Granada Hills, California, monthly 1971 to date.

INDEX

MORE GREAT READING